the growth mindset workbook for teens

say yes to challenges, deal with difficult emotions & reach your full potential

JESSICA L. SCHLEIDER, PhD
MICHAEL C. MULLARKEY, PhD
MALLORY L. DOBIAS, BS

Instant Help Books
An Imprint of New Harbinger Publications, Inc.

Publisher's Note

This publication is designed to provide accurate and authoritative information in regard to the subject matter covered. It is sold with the understanding that the publisher is not engaged in rendering psychological, financial, legal, or other professional services. If expert assistance or counseling is needed, the services of a competent professional should be sought.

Distributed in Canada by Raincoast Books

Instant Help Books
An imprint of New Harbinger Publications, Inc.
5674 Shattuck Avenue
Oakland, CA 94609
www.newharbinger.com

Cover design by Amy Shoup

Acquired by Jess O'Brien

Edited by Karen Schader

FSC www.fsc.org MIX Paper from responsible sources FSC® C011935

RAINFOREST ALLIANCE CERTIFIED

Library of Congress Cataloging-in-Publication Data

Names: Schleider, Jessica L., author. | Mullarkey, Michael C., author. | Dobias, Mallory L., author.
Title: The growth mindset workbook for teens : say yes to challenges, deal with difficult emotions, and reach your full potential / Jessica L. Schleider, Michael C. Mullarkey, and Mallory L. Dobias.
Description: Oakland, CA : Instant Help Books, [2021]
Identifiers: LCCN 2020041393 (print) | LCCN 2020041394 (ebook) | ISBN 9781684035571 (trade paperback) | ISBN 9781684035588 (pdf) | ISBN 9781684035595 (epub)
Subjects: LCSH: Emotions in adolescence--Juvenile literature. | Adjustment (Psychology) in adolescence--Juvenile literature. | Change (Psychology)--Juvenile literature. | Self-realization--Juvenile literature.
Classification: LCC BF724.3.E5 S345 2021 (print) | LCC BF724.3.E5 (ebook) | DDC 155.5/19--dc23
LC record available at https://lccn.loc.gov/2020041393
LC ebook record available at https://lccn.loc.gov/2020041394

Printed in the United States of America

23 22 21

10 9 8 7 6 5 4 3 2 1 First Printing

"This workbook is an exciting offering that leverages decades of research on people's innate power to change. Written by a team of rising stars, this workbook uses easy-to-understand language and includes many real-world examples and helpful exercises. There is something here for all teens who wish to realize their dreams, design their futures, and become the best version of themselves."

—**Bruce F. Chorpita, PhD**, professor of psychology at the University of California, Los Angeles; president of PracticeWise, LLC; and coauthor of *MATCH-ADTC*

"This is a terrific, engaging, much-needed, and practical workbook that will equip teens with powerful tools to reach their full potential. Youth will find using this book appealing, relevant, and accessible. It is full of interactive activities and thought-provoking exercises. Individuals of all ages will find this book beneficial for developing essential lifelong skills for thriving and surviving in a complicated world."

—**Golda Ginsburg, PhD**, professor of psychiatry at the University of Connecticut School of Medicine

"Jessica Schleider and colleagues have created a thoughtful, powerful, and science-guided workbook for teens who may feel 'stuck' in cycles of anxiety, depression, and stress. Their book is also the first to integrate our research on growth mindsets with brief, evidence-based treatments for youth depression and anxiety. The activities are creative, engaging, and right on-target with what science tells us can help teens cope and succeed!"

—**Carol Dweck, PhD**, Lewis and Virginia Eaton Professor in the department of psychology at Stanford University

"A gem of a book that is packed with evidence-based advice, practical strategies, and engaging material. It provides a much-needed road map for navigating the emotionally challenging teen years. I wish I had this book when I was a teen!"

—**Christopher Beevers, PhD**, Wayne H. Holztman Regents Chair in psychology, and director of the Institute for Mental Health Research at The University of Texas at Austin

"Adolescents, like all of us, have setbacks and disappointments. These may undermine mental health, or they may become opportunities for growth. This engaging, highly readable workbook—based on sound research—guides young people through the kinds of thoughts and actions needed to turn challenges into strengths. The book is a truly valuable resource for young people, as well as for parents and clinicians"

—**John R. Weisz, PhD, ABPP**, professor of psychology at Harvard University, director of the Harvard Lab for Youth Mental Health, and past president and CEO of the Judge Baker Children's Center

"This book helps you understand why you think, feel, and behave the way you do, and delivers the tools you need to change for the better or deal with what life brings you. Reading it feels less like you're in class, and more like you're with a close friend who's revealing secrets about life that you might have searched forever to discover, only your friend has a PhD from Harvard!"

—**Andres De Los Reyes, PhD**, professor of psychology at the University of Maryland, Fulbright Scholar, and editor in chief of the *Journal of Clinical Child and Adolescent Psychology*

"Schleider, Mullarkey, and Dobias bring the concept of using a 'growth mindset'—overcoming obstacles, developing desired skills, and managing one's mood effectively—to life for teens in this book. Full of useful, guided activities based on proven therapeutic strategies that work, this book will help both teens struggling with intense emotions and those that love them to follow a well-laid-out path toward achieving their goals."

—**Jill Ehrenreich-May, PhD**, professor in the department of psychology at the University of Miami, and coauthor of *Unified Protocols for Transdiagnostic Treatment of Emotional Disorders in Children and Adolescents*

To every kid, parent, and family who has taken part in our clinical research, tried out our programs, enjoyed them, hated them, and helped make them better: This workbook is for you and because of you. Thank you all so much.

Contents

a note to teens

My parents keep saying "It'll be okay" and "It'll get better"... but what if they're wrong? What if feeling bad is just part of who I am? —Katy, age 14

Katy was fed up. Half the time, she worried about saying something stupid in front of her friends; the other half, she stressed about schoolwork, which was harder this year than ever before. At home, she spent most of her time in her room, even though being alone made her feel worse—and she knew it! Katy's parents wanted to help, but no matter how many times they said "everything will be okay," Katy never really believed them. Instead, she got angry at her parents and at herself: *They don't get it. Other people can handle things, but I just can't. I'm going to feel like this forever.*

If you're like most teens, Katy's story may sound familiar. Middle and high school can feel like emotional tornadoes: totally out of control, with stress whirling in every possible direction. As therapists who work with teens (and former teenagers ourselves!), we know how hard this can be. It's tough to believe that everything will be okay when change really, truly feels impossible. It's common to feel like anger, sadness, or anxiety are just part of who you are, whether you like it or not.

This book will *not* tell you that everything will be okay. But it *will* tell you how and why you have the power to make it more okay, a little at a time.

Here's a secret that most teens, and even most adults, don't know: all of us have the ability to change our emotions, our thoughts, and the types of people we are. How do we know? Well, it turns out your power to change is a scientific fact. The human brain is a supercharged change-machine, and teen brains like yours are some of the most flexible of all. You were literally born with the ability to change.

Another powerful secret? Learning about your real power to change, or having a *growth mindset* (knowing that your traits and abilities can change), can lead you to think, feel, and act in more helpful ways. A growth mindset can help you cope with setbacks and stress, and become more like the "you" you really want to be. And guess what? A growth mindset is something you can build. It's a skill you can develop over time, just like riding a bike or playing the piano. The more you practice growth-mindset thinking, the easier it gets to talk back to your inner "I'll nevers" and "I can'ts" (*I'll never be happy; I can't get anything right*). Those messages can be overpowering. They can make you feel terrible, even when they're not at all true. But if you use your growth mindset to change them into "maybe I cans," you can rewire your brain to feel better in a way that works.

The activities in this book will teach you

- why having a growth mindset makes sense, based on the latest in brain science;
- how to grow and apply your growth mindset in order to become who you want to be, change your emotions and actions for the better, treat yourself like a good friend, *and* bounce back from stress; and
- how to use your growth mindset to work toward future goals.

Having a growth mindset is not just positive thinking, or saying "it will all be fine." A growth mindset is a powerful tool for taking action. By reminding yourself how and why change is possible, you open the door to actually *making that change a reality*. Building a growth mindset makes it possible to practice the skills you'll learn in this book—from talking back to negative thoughts to acting opposite to negative emotions. Viewing yourself as fixed, or seeing your negative emotions and thoughts as "just who you are," can chip away at your self-esteem. It can make you feel frustrated and helpless. It can trick you into thinking that nothing will ever improve, and it can even lead to depression or anxiety. The tools you will learn in this book will teach you to challenge these unhelpful thoughts and feelings. By learning about, building, and practicing a growth mindset, you will realize your true power to change.

We suggest you start off by completing Part 1 (Activities 1 through 7), "Discover Your Power to Change." This section will teach you the basics and the science of growth mindset, and it will prepare you to complete the rest of the activities in the book. (As a heads-up: you may find that Part 1 feels a bit like a science lesson, but learning the science behind *how* your brain is built to change introduces ideas that actually help you form a growth mindset.) At the end of Part 1, you will create a mindset change plan. This plan will serve as a personalized guide you can use to identify the later activities you want to try. Of course, you are welcome to complete all the activities in the book—but some may be particularly relevant to your situation or challenges.

We wish you all the best on your growth-mindset journey!

PART 1

Discover Your Power to Change

1 from brain change to self-change

for you to know

Your brain is an amazing machine. Just by reading this sentence, the building blocks of your brain, called *neurons,* are talking to each other and making thousands of new connections. In this very instant, those neurons are turning each squiggly line on this page into letters, words, and sentences—and then transforming those sentences into thoughts and ideas of your own!

Actually, your neurons have been talking to each other and forming new connections for your entire life. When you were a baby, your neurons built new connections when you took your first steps and every time you said a new word or learned to identify a new object. Over time, as you practiced and built up these skills, these neuron-to-neuron connections helped you walk, talk, and explore the world around you. Since then, they've helped you learn to do much more complicated tasks—making friends, learning to read and write, and gaining new skills like riding a bike and playing a piano.

Some skills (like learning long division) are a lot more complicated than others (like learning to flip on a light switch). Complicated skills involve *many, many* connections between neurons, and they may take more time, effort, and help from others to build. But in both cases, brain science tells us that each of us can always learn new skills, and change in all kinds of ways, through practice and effort—even when it seems impossible. Just like muscles, connections between neurons get stronger the more you use them. That means when you use your brain to complete a task, your brain "remembers" that task—and next time, the task becomes a little bit easier. The time after that, it becomes easier still … until the task is second nature.

Scientists have a special name for the brain's ability to grow, learn, and change in response to new tasks in our environment: *neuroplasticity* (pronounced *nurr-oh-plass-tiss-itty).* Neuroplasticity comes in handy every time we face a new challenge and need to learn something new—from a different way of solving a math problem to another way of getting along with a classmate. Because our brains have neuroplasticity, each of us has the ability to adapt to the changes and challenges we face.

for you to do

Think about a skill you have, or something you are good at. Try to think of something you are especially proud of. It can be a sport, like swimming or basketball; something creative, like singing, writing, or painting; or something personal, like being a good brother, sister, or friend.

What skill did you choose?

____

What makes you proudest about having this skill?

____

____

____

Thanks to neuroplasticity, skills like yours can grow and change over time. Skills are often formed from months or years of effort, setbacks, and practice.

What struggles have you faced in building your skill? Try to name at least two.

____

____

Why did you decide to keep going—continuing to build your skill in different ways—in the face of these struggles?

____

____

How have you (and your brain) learned or grown from these struggles?

____

____

Now, think back—*way* back—to when you were a little kid … the six-year-old version of yourself.

How is your skill today different from your skill when you were six?

____

____

more to do

Think about that skill you just wrote about. It might have been hard for your six-year-old self to imagine that your skill would grow into what it is today. In the space opposite, write a letter to the "younger you." In your letter, talk about

- the steps you took and the struggles you faced along the way;
- other people who helped you build your skill;
- why and how you think you managed to build that skill over time.

Remember to be kind to "younger you." You may have felt nervous about what the future holds!

To my six-year-old self,

2 changing your brain puts you in charge

for you to know

As a teenager, your brain is supercharged to learn, change, and grow in new ways. Teens have more than one hundred billion neurons to work with—not bad for a brain that weighs about as much as ten apples! What most teens don't realize is that building new connections in your brain doesn't just help with developing skills, like swimming, playing a sport, or learning the saxophone. Building new connections can also change parts of who you are, like your feelings, thoughts, and actions: how shy you are, how sad you feel, or how you cope with stress and struggles in your life.

Plus, you have a lot of control over how your brain grows and changes. You can decide the kinds of skills to develop, depending on which of your thoughts, feelings, and actions you most want to grow.

Everything you think and do helps build new connections in your brain. Believe it or not, every thought and feeling you have lives in your brain. Thoughts, by the way, are words we say to ourselves, like *I totally failed that math test* or *What if nobody likes me?* And feelings exist in our body, like fear, when our heart speeds up and we start to sweat, or sadness, when we feel heavy and tired all over. Our thoughts tend to come hand in hand with feelings. So, when someone thinks *I'll never make real friends,* they feel sadness, and a new connection forms between neurons in their brain. These connections between neurons lead to our actions in the real world.

In this case, a teenager who thinks *I'll never make real friends* or feels sadness may stay at home instead of going to school. It's tough to do much when your thoughts and feelings are so blue. Well, guess what happens in the brain when that teen stays in bed and keeps feeling sad? The connection between sadness and certain thoughts—like *I'll never make real friends*—grows even stronger. Those neurons keep talking to each other and build up larger links over time. That teen *learns* to act in certain ways (like staying home from school), even if those actions aren't what they really, truly want.

But good news: You can actually change connections between neurons. By acting differently, you can create new thoughts and feelings, which means new connections in your brain. And when neurons form new connections, your personality can change. These new connections can support different types of thoughts and feelings in response to stress. As they grow stronger, they can help you learn to cope with life's challenges in better ways.

Maria's story gives us one example:

> *Even when things feel tough, change is always possible. I learned this through my own personal experience. Last school year started out hard for me. I felt really low-energy and down all the time. Eventually, I stopped talking to other kids, I quit my soccer team, and I just stayed at home most afternoons. Somehow, I stopped doing everything that made me, well, me. It made me really sad, but I didn't feel like I had the energy for those things anymore. So I decided something had to change. First, I talked to my mom about what was going on. I also talked to a counselor at my school. We made a plan together: I would start doing three positive things every day—eat my favorite snack, go to soccer practice, and talk to at least one friend. My counselor told me that doing these things would help me build new, more positive connections in my brain. It was hard. I mean, some days I felt better, and that was awesome! But I didn't always feel up for it. Some days, I wanted to just stay in bed and do nothing all day, even though I knew that would make me feel worse. But I kept reminding myself: changing your brain is hard work, and it might take time for those new connections to stick. After a few months, I did start to feel more like myself. I wanted to do fun things. That experience taught me not to give up on myself: change is possible, even when you feel like it isn't. And support from others can go a long way in helping you change into the person you want to be.*

As Maria's story shows, people aren't stuck being sad, low-energy, or lonely. You can always change how you act, which in turn changes your thoughts and feelings. This process can help you become the person you want to be.

Everybody's brain is a work in progress.

for you to do

Everyone has moments when they feel really stressed out, or when life's struggles seem like too much to deal with. Think about the last time you felt like this. It might have been at school, around friends, or on your own.

What was going on for you during that time? Write about what happened to make that moment so stressful for you.

____

____

What is a *thought* that you had during that stressful moment? (Remember: thoughts are the things we say to ourselves—our inner voice.)

I was thinking: ___________________________

What is a *feeling* you felt during that stressful moment? (For example: sad, angry, anxious, happy, worried, calm, jealous, lonely)

Inside, I was feeling: ______________________

What were you *doing* during that stressful moment? (For example: reading a book, texting a friend, staying home, crying, laughing, doing jumping jacks)

In that stressful moment, I was: ______________

Now, think about what you've learned about the brain, personality, and people's ability to change. If this type of moment happens in the future, what could you think (or say) to yourself to remember that you (or what is happening) might change? (Remember: a thought is only helpful if you really think it's true!)

A helpful thought might be: ____

____

When you think this helpful thought, what feeling do you think you might have?

____

After thinking this helpful thought and having this feeling, what might you do differently to help yourself deal with the stress?

____

Compare and contrast the thoughts, feelings, and actions in the two examples above. What are the biggest differences?

____

____

____

If you practice the helpful thought, feeling, and action above, how do you think you might change over time? For example, do you think the thought will get easier to think? Do you think the thought might happen automatically after some practice? What would this mean for your feelings and actions?

____

____

____

more to do

Everyone's brains are constantly growing and changing, so almost everyone has a personal "change story" to tell—especially about learning to deal with stress and struggles in different ways. In this activity, we'd like you to learn more about the change story of an adult close to you.

First, pick an adult to interview (like a teacher, parent, mentor, or coach—someone you look up to). Write that person's name here:

____

Next, ask them these questions, and write down their answers.

When you were my age, what were the biggest struggles you were facing? What were some of the stressful things you were dealing with?

____

____

____

How did you deal with stress and struggles when you were my age?

____

____

____

Do you deal with struggles differently today? If so, what are the biggest differences?

What has helped you learn to deal with stress in new ways?

When you think about the new ways you've learned to deal with stress, what changes make you most proud?

If you could go back and give advice to your younger self, what would you say to let yourself know that things can change—including how you deal with stress in the future?

3 beliefs that do (and don't) boost brain change

for you to know

Teens (and adults!) tend to hold one of two types of beliefs—which brain scientists call *mindsets*—about their ability to grow, change, and bounce back after stress. These two belief types are called *fixed mindsets* and *growth mindsets.* While people with a fixed mindset tend to view personal traits like shyness, sadness, and loneliness as set in stone or near impossible to change, people with a growth mindset tend to view those same traits as changeable over time (by putting in effort, trying new strategies if needed, and finding people to support you).

Here are three important facts to know about how mindsets can shape your everyday experiences:

Fact 1: *Fixed mindsets and growth mindsets trigger very different thoughts about yourself and your ability to cope with stress.*

Fixed mindsets trigger thoughts like *You're stuck the way you are* (depressed, a "worrier," unlikable); *you will never change,* and *there's nothing you can do about it.* When you're anxious, sad, or overwhelmed—*Too bad,* a fixed-mindset thought might say. *You'd better get used to it. That's just how you are.* Fixed-mindset thoughts are exaggerated and untrue, but it's easy to fall into believing them now and then, especially when we're at our most vulnerable.

Growth mindsets trigger thoughts that tell us that change is possible, and that setbacks and stress mean opportunities for growth and change. They remind us of the scientific truth: practicing new ways of thinking helps you grow new neural connections in your brain, which opens the door for change in your feelings and actions.

Fact 2: *Mindsets tend to shift over time (from fixed to growth and back again), so almost everyone experiences both fixed- and growth-mindset thoughts at different points in time.*

You've probably had both fixed-mindset thoughts and growth-mindset thoughts before. In fact, you can have both types of thoughts in the same day (even in the same moment!). This is to be expected, because our mindsets aren't set in stone; instead, they evolve over time and are shaped by the situations we're in. For example, when you experience stress or failure, you are more vulnerable to falling into fixed-mindset thoughts—which are usually harsher and less forgiving than growth-mindset thoughts.

Fact 3: *Because they trigger such different thoughts, fixed and growth mindsets lead to very different actions.*

It's important to know the difference between your fixed- and growth-mindset thoughts, because they tell you to act in totally opposite ways.

Fixed-mindset thoughts tell you to give up when life gets tough, and to ignore or avoid things that upset you. These thoughts are the ones that tell you *Don't bother volunteering in math class; you'll just get the answer wrong and embarrass yourself* or *There's no point in going to that party; you're awful at making new friends.*

Fixed-mindset thoughts keep you in your comfort zone—so it makes sense that you'd want to listen to them. If you give up in situations where you may fall short, or pretend stressful things aren't there, you probably feel relieved … but it doesn't last long. Unfortunately, in the long run, these strategies are guaranteed to backfire. Listening to your fixed-mindset thoughts stops brain change before it even begins. The more you act in line with fixed-mindset thoughts, the less you will try out new ways of coping. You'll miss out on chances to problem solve or seek support when obstacles come your way. All of this prevents your brain from forming different connections and growing in helpful ways.

On the other hand, growth-mindset thoughts tell you that things may be tough, but you can problem solve, persevere, and seek support anyway. In other words, stress and struggle are actually opportunities for growth and change. Growth-mindset thoughts are the ones that might tell you *It may be embarrassing if I say the wrong answer in class, but my teacher can help me solve it if I don't get it right away;* or *I'm worried I'll feel alone at that party, but maybe if I practice talking to new people, it'll get a little easier.*

Listening to growth-mindset thoughts can be intimidating, because it means putting yourself in situations that are stressful (at first) or where you're not sure you'll succeed. But it also makes you more likely to learn new ways to solve problems, stand up to your fears, get the support you need, and create different brain connections when you weren't sure you could.

Fixed mindsets trigger thoughts like *I can't change, so I won't bother trying.* Listening to these thoughts makes you feel safe in the short run, but they prevent you from growing over time.

Growth mindsets trigger thoughts like *Change is hard, but it is possible, simply because of how the human brain works.* Listening to these thoughts can feel uncomfortable or scary in the short run, but they make positive change possible.

for you to do

Below are examples of setbacks that many teenagers experience. After reading Jared's story, brainstorm what a fixed mindset might say and tell each of these other teenagers to do. Then, brainstorm what a growth mindset might say and tell each to do.

Jared loses a tennis match at his first major tournament. He feels really disappointed in himself. He has team tryouts next month, but he's really not sure if he's going to get a spot on the team.

Jared's fixed mindset might say: I've proved I'm bad at tennis! There's no way I'll make the team if I didn't win this match.

And tell him: I should stay home instead of embarrassing myself at tryouts. If I stop trying, at least others won't see me fail.

Jared's growth mindset might say: After playing this match, I know there are a few things I can improve before tryouts next month. I still have a few weeks, so I bet my serve could get a lot better!

And tell him: I should see if anyone I know would be willing to practice with me this month.

Carla gets a D on a major science test. She feels devastated. There's another big test in three weeks, which gives her a chance to improve her grade in the class.

Carla's fixed mindset might say: ____

____

____

And tell her: ____

____

____

Carla's growth mindset might say: ____

____

____

And tell her: ____

____

____

It's lunchtime on the first day of school. At her last school, Kiki usually sat at a table by herself. Kiki tries to find a place to sit in the lunchroom, but she's afraid no one will want her at their table. She sees a few people from her history class at one table to her right.

Kiki's fixed mindset might say: ____

____

____

And tell her: ____

____

____

Kiki's growth mindset might say: ______________________________________

____

____

And tell her: ____

____

____

Auditions for the school play are tomorrow. Dan sees himself as a pretty shy person. He has never acted before, but he thinks it might be fun. If he does try out for the play, there's a good possibility he won't get a part.

Dan's fixed mindset might say:

____

____

And tell him:

____

____

Dan's growth mindset might say:

____

____

And tell him:

____

____

A classmate is having a big birthday party this week, and Nicholas is invited. Nicholas wants to make new friends in his grade, but he typically avoids these parties because he gets nervous talking to large groups of people.

Nicholas's fixed mindset might say:

____

____

And tell him:

____

____

Nicholas's growth mindset might say:

____

____

And tell him:

____

____

more to do

Think about a time when you were scared or nervous about doing something important to you; for example, trying out for a sports team or a play, starting a conversation with a new (potential) friend, or performing or presenting in front of an audience.

Share as many details about the situation as you can. Focus on how you were feeling, and the thoughts you were having when you were feeling the most scared or nervous.

____

____

____

____

____

Now imagine that a friend of yours is facing the same situation you just talked about.

What is a fixed-mindset thought your friend might have in that moment? (Remember: fixed-mindset thoughts tell you to give up when life gets tough, and to ignore or avoid things that upset you.)

____

____

What is a growth-mindset thought your friend might have in this moment? (Remember: growth mindset leads to thoughts like *Change is hard, but it is possible, simply because of how the human brain works.*)

____

____

What advice would you give your friend to help them listen to their growth-mindset thought instead of their fixed-mindset thought?

____

____

____

4 minding your mindsets

for you to know

So far, you have learned that your brain is capable of incredible change and growth. As you build new connections in your brain through your actions, your thoughts change as a result. This means that growth-mindset thoughts are more likely to reflect reality than fixed-mindset thoughts. Nevertheless, it's easy to fall into fixed-mindset thinking … and even start to believe those thoughts. In fact, this is an extremely common experience.

For this reason, it's critical to really get to know your own fixed-mindset thoughts. If you know how to spot them, you can talk back and stand up to them. You can replace them with growth-mindset thoughts that are truer, kinder, and *much* more helpful.

First, it's useful to start noticing situations that make you more likely to think and believe your fixed-mindset thoughts. For example, many people tend to think fixed-mindset thoughts when they are worried about making a mistake. Others notice these thoughts when they feel judged or criticized, when they are trying something hard for the first time, or when they're coping with extra life stress overall. You may notice more fixed-mindset thoughts in certain settings. For some people, school and academics can trigger lots of fixed-mindset thoughts (like *I'm stupid* or *I can't ever understand this*). For others, social settings and peers trigger more fixed-mindset thoughts (like *I just can't make real friends* or *I'm just unlikable*).

Second, fixed-mindset thoughts tend to include certain phrases that can make them easier to spot. For instance, these thoughts tend to involve lots of "I can'ts." As in *I can't do this, so there's no point in trying.* These "I can't" thoughts tell you to avoid any and all possible setbacks or challenges. Another common phrase in fixed-mindset thoughts: "I ams" (and "I'll always bes"). As in *I am a failure* (or *I am a mess, I am awful, I am unlikable*). By saying you simply "are" one way or another, these thoughts can lead you to believe that you're stuck permanently in place. This is how fixed-mindset thoughts can mask the control you really have over your actions, emotions, and thoughts.

So, to summarize: Learning to spot your fixed-mindset thoughts is a critical first step toward standing up to them. Noticing the situations and phrases connected to your own fixed-mindset thoughts is a great place to begin.

for you to do

Everyone experiences fixed- and growth-mindset thoughts at one time or another. A key step toward acting opposite to your fixed-mindset thoughts is noticing when they appear. Creating an image of your fixed mindset may help with this. It can give you some place, image, or picture of *who* and *what* you're standing up to when fixed-mindset thoughts emerge.

Name and draw your fixed mindset: the part of you that tells you to avoid and stay away from stress, to give up when things are uncertain, and to avoid things that scare you.

Name and draw your growth mindset: the part of you that reminds you that you're capable of change, even if things are hard in the moment—and the part that stands up to your fixed mindset.

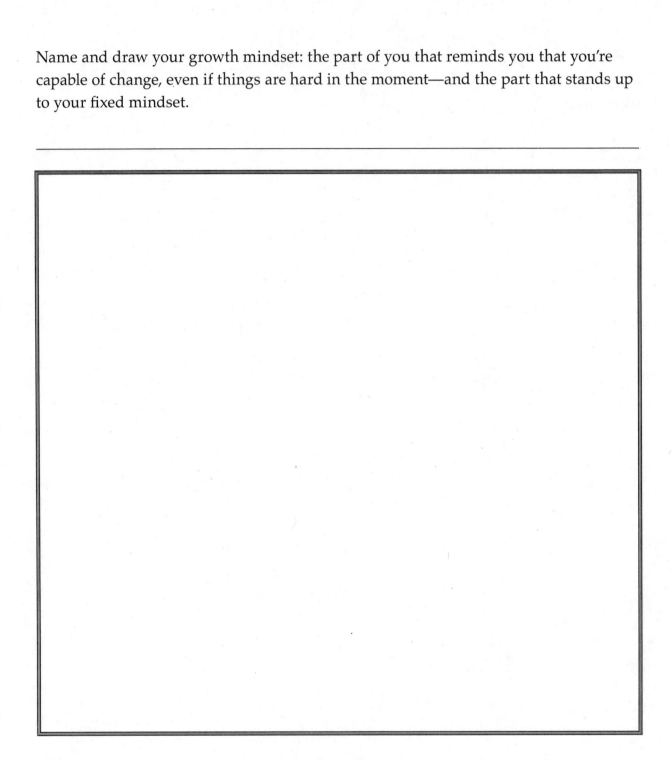

more to do

Once you have a better idea of what these fixed-mindset and growth-mindset thoughts look and sound like, it's important to figure out when and where they tend to happen for you. That's the next important step for shifting these fixed-mindset thoughts into growth-mindset thoughts.

At the website for this book, http://www.newharbinger.com/45571, you can download a log to use for keeping track of when and where you catch yourself having fixed-mindset thoughts. Print enough copies so you can track for three days, and try to do at least one thought one per day. Here's an example:

Date: October 4

Location: In the locker room

What happened? I thought about trying out for swim team, but I didn't make it last season.

What was your fixed-mindset thought? I didn't make it last time, which means I'm not a good swimmer. I can't make the team anyway, so why try?

How did you feel when this happened? I felt pretty hopeless—like I would never make the team no matter how hard I tried.

What did you end up doing? I told the coach I wasn't trying out for the team this year.

After you've kept track for three days, look back at your log, and answer these questions:

When do fixed-mindset thoughts tend to show up for you? What is happening during these times?

Where do fixed-mindset thoughts tend to show up for you? (Example: *Every time I pass the locker room by the pool.*)

Now pick one of your fixed-mindset thoughts from your log and write it down here:

What might your growth mindset say to stand up to this thought?

How do you think you would feel if you had this thought instead of what your fixed mindset told you?

____

____

What do you think you would do differently if you had this thought instead of what your fixed mindset told you?

____

____

5 from beliefs to behavior change through goals

for you to know

Knowing your power to change and spotting your fixed-mindset thoughts are two critical steps toward positive everyday change. But how do you make the jump from "knowing" to "acting" toward the change you hope to see?

This activity will share some key steps to creating the changes you care about—specifically, by setting growth-mindset goals and making action plans for achieving them.

Growth-mindset goals have these important features.

They are stated positively. Focus on how you would most like to grow, act, or improve, instead of what you want to stop doing or feeling. For example, "I want to become *less* lonely" is a negatively stated goal; "I want to connect with people *more* by texting one good friend every day" is a positively stated goal. It's pretty hard to take action toward that negative goal, but the positive goal creates a clearer path toward change.

They set you up to ACT when they are **a**chievable, **c**oncrete, and **t**rackable so you can tell when you've met them. Ask yourself these questions to check if your goal fits the ACT targets:

- Is your goal achievable? In other words, can you reach this goal in the near future? Many teens find it easiest to think about long-term, large, and faraway goals, like "I want to be successful in life" or "I want to make a difference in the world." These are great goals but, in reality, reaching them means first reaching many (many!) smaller goals over time. Shifting your focus to smaller, in-between goals can help you take real steps toward long-term change.

- Is your goal concrete? Is it focused and specific enough for you to take action toward achieving it? (Example: "I would like to practice piano three times a week this month" instead of "I want to be a better musician.") Making your goals more concrete gives you a better idea of how to get where you want to be.
- Is your goal trackable? Can you keep track of whether you have made the concrete changes you planned, at the *times* you planned to make them? (Example: "I'll offer to help my mother out twice each weekend" instead of "I want to improve my relationship with my family this year.") Setting trackable goals makes it easier to tell when you've accomplished what you've set out to do.

They need to matter to you. They should reflect what you care about—whether that is connecting with friends or family, being kinder to yourself, or trying a new challenge. This helps you stay motivated to achieve them.

They involve a plan for spotting and coping with obstacles. Making change is challenging, and setbacks are part of the process. Sticking to growth-mindset goals means problem solving obstacles instead of avoiding them—by seeking support from others and thinking of new solutions—to get back on track and make the change you care about.

So overall, growth-mindset goals are stated positively, help you act, focus on what matters to you, and include problem-solving plans for when setbacks emerge. This may sound complicated, but creating growth-mindset goals takes practice, and struggles and setbacks are often part of the process.

for you to do

It can be tricky to create growth-mindset goals at first, but it gets much easier with practice. Read these examples, and then help each of the teenagers below create a growth-mindset goal that sets them up to act.

Aaron's goal: *I don't want to make a D in science class anymore.*

Rephrase Aaron's goal so it is stated positively: I want to do well in science class.

Is Aaron's new goal achievable in the near future? Tell why, or why not. Doing well in the class might be a longer-term goal. There are other interim goals to work toward, like setting up and keeping to a study schedule, before he reaches that long-term goal.

If Aaron's goal is not achievable, rewrite it to be more achievable: I will get help from my science teacher.

Is Aaron's new goal concrete? Tell why, or why not. "Getting help" from his science teacher is not very specific and could mean many different things.

If Aaron's goal is not concrete, rewrite it to be more concrete: I will get help from my science teacher during office hours.

Is Aaron's new goal trackable? Tell why, or why not. No, because his goal isn't specific about how often or how many times he's hoping to get help from his teacher during office hours.

If Aaron's goal is not trackable, rewrite it to be more trackable: I will get help from my science teacher during office hours once a week.

Why do you think Aaron's goal matters to him? Aaron wants to improve his grades in science class so he can feel better about how he's doing in school.

Name two people who can help Aaron with his goal, and tell how they can help:

1. His science teacher can help him during office hours.
2. His friend Caleb can encourage him to visit during office hours, even if he doesn't want to one week.

Now help these other teenagers create growth-mindset goals.

Macy's goal: *I want to feel less isolated from other people.*

Rephrase Macy's goal so it is stated positively: ______________________________

____

____

Is Macy's new goal achievable in the near future? Tell why, or why not. ______________

____

____

If Macy's goal is not achievable, rewrite it to be more achievable: ________________

____

____

Is Macy's new goal concrete? Tell why, or why not. ______________________________

____

____

If Macy's goal is not concrete, rewrite it to be more concrete: ____________________

____

____

Is Macy's new goal trackable? Tell why, or why not. ____________________

____

____

If Macy's goal is not trackable, rewrite it to be more trackable: ____________________

____

____

Why do you think Macy's goal matters to her?

____

____

Name two people who can help Macy with her goal, and tell how they can help:

1. ____
2. ____

Will's goal: *I want to be less shy in class.*

Rephrase Will's goal so it is stated positively: ______________________________

____

____

Is Will's new goal achievable in the near future? Tell why, or why not. __________

____

____

If Will's goal is not achievable, rewrite it to be more achievable: ______________

____

____

Is Will's new goal concrete? Tell why, or why not. __________________________

____

____

If Will's goal is not concrete, rewrite it to be more concrete: __________________

____

____

Is Will's new goal trackable? Tell why, or why not. ______________________________

____

____

If Will's goal is not trackable, rewrite it to be more trackable: ________________

____

____

Why do you think Will's goal matters to him?

____

____

Name two people who can help Will with his goal, and tell how they can help:

1. ____

2. ____

more to do

Now that you've practiced helping others create their growth mindset goals, let's try it out on a goal you would like to reach.

Write down a goal that matters a lot to you. Make sure it is positively stated, achievable, concrete, and trackable.

____

____

Circle the part of the goal that makes it a positive statement.

Draw a box around the part of the goal that makes it achievable.

Place a star next to the part of the goal that makes it concrete.

Underline the part of the goal that makes it trackable.

Setbacks often happen when we try to reach our goals. Name two people who can help with your goal when things get tough, and tell how they can help.

1. ____

2. ____

Now that you have your growth-mindset goal, use this log (or download a copy at http://www.newharbinger.com/45571) to track your progress toward your goal for the next five days.

Day	What I did to move toward my goal	What I thought (including any growth-mindset thoughts)	How I felt
1			
2			
3			
4			
5			

working toward the experiences you want, fast and slow

6

for you to know

So far, this book has focused a lot on change, including your power to

change your own behaviors, thoughts, and feelings;

talk back when fixed-mindset thoughts tell you change can't happen; and

set growth-mindset goals that help you take action.

But there are other questions, just as important, that we haven't covered yet: How do you cope when change doesn't happen as fast as you'd like? Or when you seem to be getting further away from your goal, not closer, despite your best efforts?

First of all, you're not alone. Anyone who tries to change their actions, thoughts, or feelings is taking a risk—and that can be scary. You are being brave just by working toward change to begin with.

Second, setbacks are unavoidable when you're making difficult changes. And knowing that setbacks are coming doesn't always make them easier to cope with.

We asked a few teens for their advice on how they have coped when change happens slowly (or goes in the wrong direction):

Cut yourself some slack. (Emilia, age 17)

You won't be perfect. Mistakes are only human, so you can cut yourself some slack, just like you would for anybody else who was struggling. Beating up on yourself won't make change happen faster. I know, because I've done it. The fact is that your goal probably means a lot to you, so it's worth trying to find a different solution. Mistakes just tell you what not to try next. Just because one thing didn't work, that doesn't mean nothing will.

Look back on how far you've come. (Jackson, age 16)

In seventh grade I pronounced a word wrong when I was reading out loud in class. It wasn't even a hard word—"magnet"—but I completely messed it up, and some kids started laughing at me and wouldn't stop. I pretty much stopped talking in class after that. I felt so stupid. There were days I faked being sick to avoid going to school at all. I hated being so anxious all the time. So when I got to high school, I wanted a fresh start. I started meeting with the school counselor, and she helped me cope with my anxiety better, to talk back to it more. I guess there's still room to improve, because my teachers still tell me to participate more. But I'm honestly okay with being at school now, and I raise my hand at least sometimes. I'm really proud of where I'm at compared to where I was before.

Give yourself time. (Cora, age 16)

I'm not sure why but starting conversations with people has always been really stressful for me, even with close friends. I get nervous I'll say something dumb, or people will think the topics I like are weird. Even though it's uncomfortable, I've been trying to start more conversations this year, at least with my friends. You know, just go for it, because I know things get easier the more you practice. When I've managed to do it, things definitely went better than I expected. But sometimes I just feel too nervous, so I stay quiet. When that happens, I tend to get mad at myself … like, I'm really trying, so why is this still so hard? But then again, I've had this problem since I was a kid. That's more than half my life! It seems fair to give myself some time to get used to a whole new way of doing things.

Ask for support. (Jacqui, age 17)

> *Sometimes you just need a boost from someone who cares about you. Tenth grade was hard for me. I felt like I couldn't do anything right, like I just wasn't good enough. I tried to distract myself and just think more positively, but these sad feelings kept coming back. At some point—honestly by accident—I ended up telling a friend what was going on. I try to keep these things to myself because I don't like to bother people with my problems. But it felt so, so good to tell her about it. She really got what I was going through. It turns out she had a similar experience and had ideas for who I could talk to and strategies that helped her in the past. It helped to know there were ways to cope I hadn't tried yet. Plus, it was a relief not to feel so alone.*

Obstacles and struggles will happen regardless. What matters most is how you choose to respond to them. By learning which of these four strategies works best for you when changes are challenging or slow, you can set yourself up to cope effectively—and persevere anyway.

for you to do

Let's figure out *which* of these four strategies works best for you, and *when* it might be most helpful in your day-to-day life.

Circle the strategy you think would be most effective:

cutting yourself some slack

looking back on how far you've come

giving yourself time

asking for support

Why do you think this one would be most effective?

____

____

If you *have* used one of these strategies before:

When did it best help you cope with slower change?

____

____

When did this strategy not help you cope with slower change?

____

____

If you *have not* used one of these strategies before:

Are there any situations where you think your top strategy would not help you cope with slower change? Why?

___

___

When do you think your top strategy would be most helpful in coping with slower change? Why?

___

___

more to do

Now that you've identified *which* strategy would work best for you, and *when* you'll likely benefit from it most, let's try it out!

For the next three days,. use this tracker (or download a copy at http://www.newharbinger.com/45571). Write down how you were feeling just before, and just after, trying out your strategy. If you notice your feelings aren't changing after using your top strategy, try out a different strategy the next day.

Day	Strategy I used	How I felt just before using this strategy	How I felt just after using this strategy
1			
2			
3			

Did you use the same strategy on all three days? Yes No

If you used one strategy, did it work better for some situations for than for others? Explain.

____

____

____

____

If you used different strategies, which strategy seemed to work best for you?

____

____

7 your mindset change plan

for you to know

Setbacks, failures, and losses are unavoidable parts of being a teenager, and coping with them is no easy task. In high-pressure and stressful moments, it's natural to slip into fixed-mindset thinking. You may notice your mind landing on thoughts like *I can't handle this,* or *I'll never be good enough*—so often that you start to believe it. You may get stuck on what you think is *wrong* with yourself, what you *can't* change, or how you will *always* be.

We've written this book to help you break free from this kind of thinking—and remember that none of those thoughts are really true. In fact, neuroscience tells us the exact opposite: you have built-in potential to change how you think, what you do, and the connections in your brain, all of which make up who you are. The activities in the upcoming sections of this book are meant to help you become your very best, in ways that feel most important to you. Overall, they are designed to help you:

catch fixed-mindset thinking right when it happens;

replace unrealistic fixed-mindset thoughts with realistic growth-mindset thoughts;

act in ways that follow naturally from growth-mindset thoughts; and

repeat this process—catch, replace, act—to grow and change in ways you care about.

As an added bonus: In many of the book sections, you will learn how cutting-edge brain science explains *why* and *how* these activities can lead to self-change that matters to you. Not only will you gain strategies for helping yourself work toward growth, but you'll also become prepared to support others in their change journey.

As you work your way through different activities, you may find some of them challenging. You'll be asked to problem solve and think in ways that may feel uncomfortable, unnatural, or even anxiety provoking. If you notice that an activity is especially difficult, *that is a good sign.* It means you're exercising and creating totally new connections in your brain and working toward the change you're hoping to achieve.

Working through these activities will take commitment. You will have to pay close attention to your thoughts and really stick with each activity you start. This can be scary, and sometimes even discouraging, if things don't go as planned. But that is all part of the change process. We know your commitment will pay off.

Two things are especially important to know as you move further in this book. First, to keep yourself on track (and tune into whether an activity is helping) it's helpful to know *how* and *why* you hope to change and grow. Second, because everyone's hopes and challenges are different, some activities in this book will be more relevant to you than others. The next few pages will help you start to identify what your hopes are—and which activities might be the best starting points for working toward reaching them.

for you to do

To identify your hopes for using this book, it can be helpful to think first about the inner obstacles that may get in your way.

Which of these inner obstacles seem relevant to you? Check all that apply.

- ☐ **It's hard to believe you can change.** You're still not convinced that things could get better for you, even if you think that others can probably change.
- ☐ **It's hard to stand up to your inner "I can'ts."** Your fixed-mindset thoughts are pretty loud and very frequent. It's hard to imagine getting past all that negative self-talk.
- ☐ **It's hard to figure out what your goals are.** You're not sure where to begin thinking about goals for yourself—but you know that your coping skills could improve in some way.
- ☐ **It's hard to get yourself going.** Even though you want to change, it seems like *so* much work; you're tired just thinking about it. Maybe it's just too much.
- ☐ **It's hard to be kind to yourself.** You are often self-critical, and you worry about what might happen if you were easier on yourself.
- ☐ **It's hard to ask for help.** You want to be able to handle things on your own, so you tend not to turn to others, even if you know they might be able to help.
- ☐ **It's hard to bounce back after stress and/or failure.** You're just not sure when to start. Falling short is really tough, and it's hard to feel okay after it happens.

Pick your top two inner obstacles—perhaps the ones you think will get in your way the most or the ones you most want to overcome. Put a check next to those two obstacles, and decide on your hope for each of them. We've provided a hope commonly linked to each of these obstacles; you can also write in your own hope.

Obstacle: It's hard to believe you can change.

Hope: To find my growth mindset

OR, write in your own hope:____

Obstacle: It's hard to stand up to your inner "I can'ts."

Hope: To notice, and stand up to, my fixed-mindset thoughts

OR, write in your own hope:____

Obstacle: It's hard to figure out what your goals are.

Hope: To identify my values and activities consistent with these values

OR, write in your own hope:____

Obstacle: It's hard to get yourself going.

Hope: To plan time to do things I value; to act on what I care about

OR, write in your own hope:____

Obstacle: It's hard to be kind to yourself (or you are often self-critical).

Hope: To learn to practice self-kindness (especially after setbacks)

OR, write in your own hope:____

Obstacle: It's hard to ask for help.

Hope: To identify supportive people in my life, and practice reaching out

OR, write in your own hope:____

Obstacle: It's hard to bounce back after stress and/or failure.

Hope: To learn from setbacks to plan for future success

OR, write in your own hope:____

Okay, now you have your two hopes. Write them down:

Hope 1: ____

Hope 2: ____

Why are these hopes so important to you?

____

____

____

____

Now that you've identified your top two obstacles and hopes, you can use the following guide to find (and circle) the activities in this book that are most relevant to you and your life. Although all the activities can help, we encourage you to be sure to try the suggestions in the third column.

Obstacle(s)	Part(s)	Activities
It's hard to believe you can change. It's hard to stand up to your inner "I can'ts."	2, 4	8, 10, 11, 15, 16, 17
It's hard to figure out what your goals are. It's hard to get yourself going.	2	9, 10, 11
It's hard to be kind to yourself (or you are often self-critical).	3, 4	12, 13, 14, 15, 16, 17
It's hard to ask for help.	4, 5	15, 17, 19, 20
It's hard to bounce back after stress and/or failure.	4, 5	16, 17, 18, 19, 20

more to do

As you work your way through this book, you can gauge progress toward your hopes by keeping track of how "big" these top obstacles are in your life.

Think about the first obstacle you listed above. On a scale from 0 (it's the biggest problem in my life) to 10 (I'm totally over it), where are you today for this obstacle?

____

Where on this scale would you like to be? Which number would be most manageable for you?

____

How would your life be different if you were at this number?

Now, think about the second obstacle you listed above. Using the same scale, where are you today for this obstacle?

____

Where on this scale would you like to be? Which number would be most manageable for you?

____

How would your life be different if you were at this number?

____

____

____

____

You can revisit this ratings scale to keep track of your progress—and see if you're getting closer to a number that's manageable for you.

PART 2

Become Who You Hope to Be, Especially When Life Gets Hard

8 standing up to your "I can't" mindset

for you to know

So far, you have gotten to know what your inner "I can'ts" and "I'm just nots" look like and sound like, along with where and when they tend to show up. These are great steps, but you're still left with a key question: What can you *do* about your fixed-mindset thoughts once you catch them?

Fixed-mindset thoughts tend to come up when you're facing stress, worry, or challenge. Like when you're asked to do something you don't feel confident about; when you've put yourself out there and risked being judged; when you feel alone, scared, or lonely. It's important to know that you are most vulnerable to buying into your own negative thoughts during these high-stress moments, because standing up to your fixed mindset takes effort … but setbacks and stressors can leave your brain and body exhausted. They can leave you with less energy to stand up to your fixed mindset when you need to the most.

The result? A real challenge: fixed-mindset thoughts tend to come up when you face stress, *and* stress makes you more vulnerable to believing your false fixed-mindset thoughts. And the good news? The challenge is solvable. You have the power to plan and practice how you'll stand up to fixed-mindset thoughts in advance. By thinking through exactly how you'll stand up to these thoughts, and practicing your steps before new challenges emerge, you're doing an amazing favor for Future You. You're making it easier and more automatic to stand up to negative thoughts when things get tough.

How do you get ready to stand up to your "I can'ts" and "I'll nevers" in the future? Two steps can help:

Step 1: Write down your negative fixed-mindset thought. This can be a thought you've had before, one you might have in the future, or something you're thinking right now. For example, *I'll always be bad at making friends.* After writing it down, find what makes it a fixed-mindset thought. Does it include "I can't" or "I'll always/never be"?

Step 2: Rewrite your negative thought into a helpful growth-mindset thought by changing the beginning and the end. For example, you might add "My fixed mindset is telling me …" to the beginning of your thought, and "that fixed-mindset thought is mean, but it may not be right because …" to the end. (Remember: your inner thoughts tell *your* story, and you can rewrite your story however you choose.)

Step 2 is a little trickier than Step 1, but it just takes some practice before it feels natural. Tory, age 14, shared one experience of using these steps in her life:

> *Yesterday I texted a girl I'm hoping to be friends with, but she didn't text me back. I caught myself thinking mean things, like how I'm weird and bad at making friends, which was for sure my fixed mindset talking. I still sort of believe those thoughts sometimes, but I know they don't get me anywhere. So I tried to rewrite it like I'd practiced.*
>
> *First I wrote it down and circled the parts that made it fixed, like "I'm weird" and "I'm bad at making friends." That made it easy to see the parts that can't be totally true, since nobody is stuck one way forever. Next I added a new beginning to the thought: "My fixed mindset is saying that I'm weird and bad at making friends." After that, it felt less like I was yelling at myself. It was just my fixed mindset talking. Then I added a different ending, which was the same one I came up with during practice: "That thought is mean, but it's not right. Things will get better than they are right now." I also added an extra part: "I have a couple of good friends so I can't be that bad at making them!" Rewriting the thought didn't fix everything. But it helped me feel more okay. I knew things could change, so at least there was more hope than before.*

Fixed-mindset thoughts are natural. In fact, they're impossible to avoid. But by planning and practicing how you'll cope with them in the future, you can prepare yourself to deal with them when they *do* come up—and help yourself take charge of your own thoughts and story.

for you to do

Practice standing up to fixed-mindset thoughts that other teenagers have shared with us.

> Joy, age 15, has gotten mostly As and Bs in her history course so far. On a recent quiz, however, she got a C-. She thinks, *How could I let this happen? I suck at school.*

Step 1. Circle the parts that make Joy's thought fixed.

How do you think Joy would feel after having this thought?

____

What do you think Joy would do in response to this thought?

____

Step 2. Rewrite the thought by adding a new beginning and a new ending:__________

____

____

How do you think Joy would feel in response to this new thought?

____

What do you think Joy would do in response to this new thought?

___

Alex, age 16, finds out that some of his friends went to the movies without him last weekend. He thinks, *This always happens to me. I'll never have true friends.*

Step 1. Circle the parts that make Alex's thought fixed.

How do you think Alex would feel after having this thought?

___

What do you think Alex would do in response to this thought?

___

Step 2. Rewrite the thought by adding a new beginning and a new ending: ___

___

___

How do you think Alex would feel in response to this new thought?

___

What do you think Alex would do in response to this new thought?

___

more to do

Choose an area of your life that has caused you worry, stress, or sadness. Now, think of a situation in that area that has created one of those difficult emotions. Try to pick a situation that comes up regularly—something you will probably have to deal with in the future—and that might lead to fixed-mindset thoughts for you. (Feel free to refer back to Activity 6 if you're having trouble thinking of examples.)

Academics (Examples: worry about an upcoming exam; feeling overwhelmed by schoolwork; falling behind in class)

What situation did you choose?

____

Peers (Examples: trying to make new friends; arguments with friend group; worrying what others think about you)

What situation did you choose?

____

Many teens experience difficult emotions around academics and peers, but there are other areas that may also be challenging; for example, family relationships or work situations.

What area has been difficult for you?

____

What situation did you choose?

____

Now write down what happened the last time you were in a stressful situation like the one you wrote about above.

What was the situation?

____

Who were you with?

____

Where and when did it happen?

____

How did you feel during this situation?

____

What fixed-mindset thought did you have during this situation? Try to write down the whole thought that bothered you, from beginning to end.

____

____

Circle the parts of your thought that made it fixed.

Now, rewrite the thought to make it more helpful, by adding a new beginning and a new end. (Remember: a rewritten thought is *only helpful if you really believe it.*)

know your values 9

for you to know

You've now learned about why you have the power to change (because of your brain's potential for growth) and strategies for standing up to fixed-mindset thoughts that get in your way. But how do you decide which changes to strive for? What steps can you take that will make the biggest impact on your day-to-day life? How do you grow into the "you" you want to be?

Everyone has different answers to these questions. To figure out yours, it helps to start by identifying your personal values: the things that matter most to you in everyday life and help give your life meaning. Relationships, courage, honesty, and education are all examples of personal values. Your values reflect what you care about, what you stand for, and what you consider to be truly important, and they are different for everybody. When people are able to act on their personal values, they feel most like their true and best selves.

Living by your values might sound easy to do. Your values are the things that are most important to you, after all. It should be natural to live by them—right?

In reality, living by your values is much easier said than done. In this activity, you'll take the first steps to learn what values mean and which values matter the most to you. This will help you figure out *how* you most hope to grow and feel most like the true "you" in the future.

How do values differ from goals? Values are *directions* we want to keep moving toward. Living by your values is a lot like traveling west: no matter how far you go, you can never actually get there. It's a direction, not a destination. Goals are what we want to *achieve* along the way. They are more like landmarks—specific rivers, mountains, or valleys you hope to cross while traveling in your chosen direction.

For example, if you care about being a dedicated, motivated student and learner, that's a value you can live by each day. Living by this value is an ongoing process. In contrast, graduating from high school is a goal. It's something you can cross off your to-do list once you achieve it. Once you've graduated from high school, you are done—*even* if you continue to improve as a student and learner afterward (for example, in college). Being a motivated student and learner is an ongoing process, with no clear end point. That's how you know it's a value rather than a goal.

Why does it help to know your personal values? The first step to acting on your values—using your values to guide your actions—is figuring out what they are. Acting on your values allows you to grow your favorite parts of yourself—the parts you truly like, and the parts that really matter. Knowing your values can help you stand up to—and act opposite to—your fixed-mindset thoughts. By knowing and living by your values, you can take control of your life's direction, choosing each day to become the person you hope to become.

One last thing to note before you move on to the next part of this activity: your values can actually change over time, based on your situation, and the ways you change as a person over the course of your life. The fact that your values can (and do—and probably already have!) change will be helpful to keep in mind as you go through the rest of this activity.

for you to do

There are hundreds of values a person can have, and each value can have different meanings for different people. Some common values are listed in the image below. Some of them may matter more to you than others. If you think of a value that's not already listed, you can add it to the "My Own Value" box. There are no "right" or "wrong" values to hold. The key is finding out which ones are important to you.

For each of these values, first write down what that value *means* to you.

Next, rate how important that value is to you—both *today* and *five years ago*—on a scale from 0 (not at all important) to 10 (the most important).

Examples of describing a value:

> "Relationships" might mean …
>
> > "Spending lots of time with people I care about" to one person, and
> >
> > "Being supportive when my friends need me" to another.
>
> "Health" might mean …
>
> > "Taking care of my body by exercising" to one person, and
> >
> > "Doing activities I like to stay happy and healthy" to another.

Any value description that feels right to you is the one you should use.

HEALTH

To me, this value means:

Importance today? (0–10)

Importance five years ago?

FAMILY

To me, this value means:

Importance today? (0–10)

Importance five years ago?

EDUCATION, WISDOM

To me, this value means:

Importance today? (0–10)

Importance five years ago?

COMPASSION, HELPING

To me, this value means:

Importance today? (0–10)

Importance five years ago?

RELATIONSHIPS

To me, this value means:

Importance today? (0–10)

Importance five years ago?

PLEASURE, ENJOYMENT

To me, this value means:

Importance today? (0–10)

Importance five years ago?

SPIRITUALITY, RELIGION

To me, this value means:

Importance today? (0–10)

Importance five years ago?

PERSEVERENCE

To me, this value means:

Importance today? (0–10)

Importance five years ago?

INDEPENDENCE

To me, this value means:

Importance today? (0–10)

Importance five years ago?

COMMUNITY

To me, this value means:

Importance today? (0–10)

Importance five years ago?

MY OWN VALUE:

____

To me, this value means:

Importance today? (0–10)

Importance five years ago?

Now circle the three values that matter the most to you today. For each value, tell why it is important to you. Then write down something related to this value that you can do in the next twenty-four hours (your immediate goal), something you can do in the next week (your short-term goal), and something you can do in the next year or two (your long-term goal). Finally, if the value has changed in importance over time—whether it has gotten more or less important—tell why you think this change occurred. You can skip this step if the value hasn't changed.

Value 1: ____

Why it is important to you: ______________________________

____

Your immediate goal: __________________________________

____

Your short-term goal: __________________________________

____

Your long-term goal: ___________________________________

____

If this value has changed over time, why do you think the change occurred?

____

____

Value 2: ____

Why it is important to you: ____________________________________

____

Your immediate goal: ____________________________________

____

Your short-term goal: ____________________________________

____

Your long-term goal: ____________________________________

____

If this value has changed over time, why do you think the change occurred?

____

____

Value 3: ____

Why it is important to you: ________________________________

____

Your immediate goal: ______________________________________

____

Your short-term goal: _____________________________________

____

Your long-term goal: ______________________________________

____

If this value has changed over time, why do you think the change occurred?

____

____

more to do

Choose one of these three values to focus on:______________________________

Think about a specific time in your life when you got to really express or act on this value. In answering the questions that follow, include as much detail as you can.

Describe any obstacles you encountered in expressing or acting on your value:

____

____

How did you express your value (for example, what actions did you take), and how did you feel after doing so?

____

____

What were you thinking about while expressing this value?

____

____

How did other people react when you acted on your value?

____

____

Now think about upcoming events and situations in your own life. Try to identify one opportunity you might have to act on this value in the near future (for example, the next week). And again, include as much detail as possible.

When will this opportunity happen?

____

____

Where will it be?

____

____

Who, if anybody, will be with you?

____

____

Name one person who can help remind you to act on this value:

____

10 act on your values to fight fixed thoughts

for you to know

Once you know what your values are, you can start to act on them. By acting on your values, you can stand up to fixed-mindset thoughts that hold you back, and you can grow the parts of yourself you care about most. You can use your values to guide your actions.

Your values can motivate you to stand up to negative thinking, including fixed-mindset thoughts, when doing so feels difficult. You've already learned that fixed thinking tend to happen during high-stress moments. Unfortunately, stress can easily make us feel distracted, tired, and overwhelmed—which all make it especially hard to rewrite negative thoughts into truthful, helpful ones. Sometimes you'll need a boost. It can help to think about your values in these moments—and turn rewriting fixed thoughts into opportunities to act on your values.

If your top value is kindness, rewriting fixed thoughts could be a chance for you to show kindness to yourself. Perhaps you value honesty; by challenging false, fixed self-talk, you can help your thoughts reflect what's true. Or maybe you care most about close relationships; in this case, challenging fixed thoughts might give you the mental space you need to be present with friends.

In short, standing up to fixed negative thoughts can be your way of acting on your values, and being the type of person you want to be.

Rosie, age 13, shared an example of how knowing her values helps her combat fixed thinking:

> *One value I care about is perseverance—sticking with something until you figure out a solution. It's important to me because my mom has struggled a lot in life, but she somehow finds a way through hard times. I admire that about her. So, recently I've dealt with a lot of bad thoughts, like I'll never be good enough, smart enough or whatever … usually after I mess up. But I know those thoughts aren't true; they're just fixed ideas from my brain. When they happen, I just try to tell myself, "You can find a way through this. You're your mom's daughter." Like, reminding myself that I really am somebody who can persevere and find a way through. Or at least I can try, just like my mom would.*

By remembering your values, you can help yourself fight fixed thinking—while *also* being the person you really want to be.

for you to do

From time to time, you may be in a position to help others in your life cope with their own fixed-mindset thoughts. For instance, a friend or family member might share that they are feeling down or discouraged about their ability to succeed, change, or grow.

Think about a time when you helped someone in your life cope with a difficult thought or feeling.

Who did you help? ____

What was the situation?

____

____

How did you feel after you helped them?

____

What values did you act on by helping them? Circle two from the following list, or add others on the blank lines:

- Kindness
- Courage
- Independence
- Wisdom
- Compassion
- Perseverance
- Health
- Other: ____________________
- Other: ____________________
- Other: ____________________

How did you act on them by helping this person in your life?

I acted on the first value, ____________________, by doing/saying ____________________.

I acted on the second value, ________________, by doing/saying ________________.

In the future, when your own fixed thoughts come up, you can act on these same values in order to help yourself.

Do you think helping yourself will be easier or harder than helping others? Why?

____

____

____

____

In the future, what is one thing you can say to yourself to make it easier to help yourself?

____

more to do

Practice acting on your values when fixed thoughts come up this week. First, pick two values to act on toward yourself:

Value 1: ____

How will you act on this value to help yourself through fixed thoughts?

I will tell myself: ____

One action I can take is: ____

Value 2: ____

How will you act on this value to help yourself through fixed thoughts?

I will tell myself: ____

One action I can take is: ____

Next, try to catch yourself acting on your values in response to fixed thinking. See if you can do this twice in the next week.

Here's an example:

Date: April 15 **Time of day:** 8:00 p.m.

What was the situation? My little sister had a bad argument with her best friend. She was so upset and sad, and I didn't know how to help her even though I wanted to.

What was your fixed thought? I'm the worst sister. I don't know how to help her when she needs me.

Which value did you act on toward yourself? And how? Compassion. I told myself that I don't automatically need to know how to help her, but I can still try. I also showed compassion to my sister by telling her that I was there for her.

How did it go? It went well! It turned out that just me being there with her made her feel a little better. It made me feel better, too.

Now it's your turn.

Situation 1

Date: ______________________________ Time of day: __________________

What was the situation? ____

____

____

What was your fixed thought? (Circle the parts that made it fixed.)

____

____

____

Which value did you act on toward yourself? And how?

____

____

____

How did it go?

____

____

____

Situation 2

Date: ______________________________ Time of day: ________________

What was the situation? ____

____

____

What was your fixed thought? (Circle the parts that made it fixed.)

____

____

____

Which value did you act on toward yourself? And how?

____

____

____

How did it go?

____

____

____

11 act on your values to master your mood

for you to know

Your choices about how you act, including whether and when to act on your values, can do more than help you fight off unhelpful fixed thinking. They can also change how you feel—for better or for worse, including after you've gone through stress and setbacks.

Take 16-year-old Kat's story as an example:

> *I've played volleyball since I was eight years old. It's always been my favorite thing. Last year, I decided to try out for my school's varsity team. My best friend made it, but I got cut. I felt sick when I found out. My friend was nice about it, but I was just so mad at myself. I felt stupid for thinking I could make it. After that, things got tough. I just wanted to hide. Hanging out with my friend, being at school—it all seemed like too much. I didn't have energy for anything, not even the things I really cared about. I felt really low during that time. I didn't understand what was happening. I remember thinking,* will I ever feel like myself again?

Kat's story is actually very common. To understand why, it's helpful to revisit how your brain works. Stressful events (like getting cut from the volleyball team) trigger an automatic "must avoid!" response in the human brain. This part of the brain helped early humans stay safe. (It helped us avoid getting eaten by wooly mammoths!) And sometimes, it still does protect you from danger (for example, by telling you to wait until traffic stops before crossing a busy street). But other times, our brain can get things wrong. It can stay in "must avoid!" mode for longer than we need—even after the "danger," or stressful event, is long gone.

In Kat's case, her brain actually made a mistake: it told her to keep avoiding for *too long* ... which led her to fall into a negative mood spiral. She started to feel sad and unmotivated to do things she values—even things that had nothing to do with volleyball.

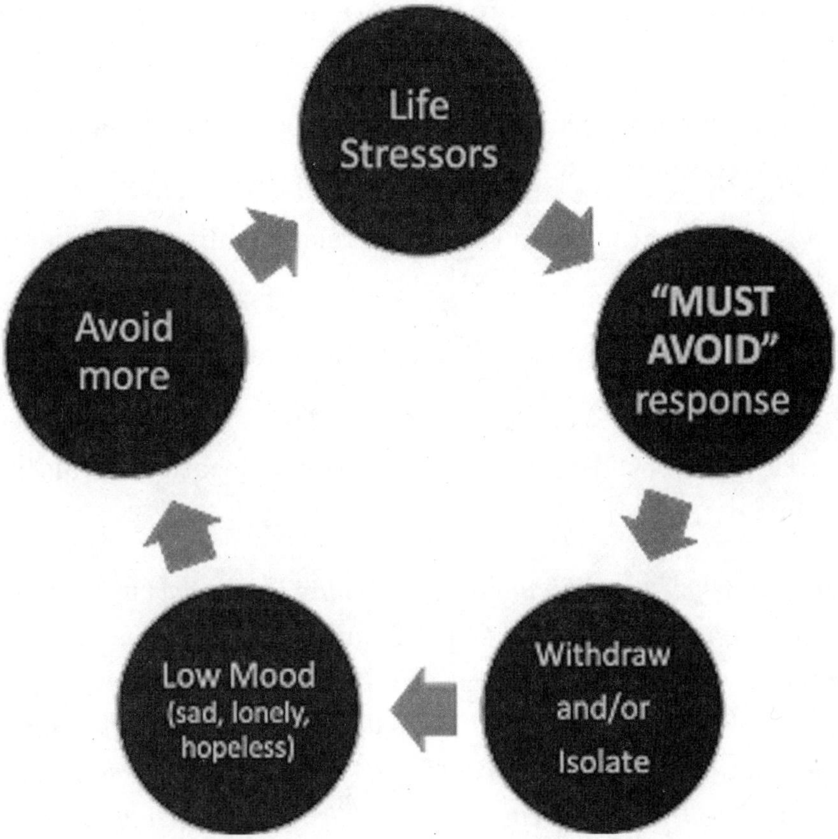

The more stress you experience, the harder it gets to enjoy things you once loved, and the easier it gets to fall into one of these spirals. This happens to lots of teens; in fact, at some point before turning eighteen, one out of every five teenagers in the United States falls into a negative mood spiral lasting for two weeks or longer.

The good news is that you can reverse your negative spirals simply by acting on your values. Research shows that at least three types of value-based actions can help reverse negative spirals:

- Connecting with people who make you feel good (some related values: relationships, community, compassion)
- Achieving goals that matter to you (some related values: perseverance, education, wisdom)
- Enjoying activities on your own (some related values: pleasure, health, independence)

After learning that value-based action can help reverse negative spirals, here's what Kat did to cope in a better way:

> *At first I wasn't sure how to act on my values. I hadn't thought about it before. The only thing I could think of was, I don't know … doing stuff that reminded me of me. It almost sounded too simple, but that's what I started to do. I started focusing more on my photography. I think it's really important to see the beauty in the world. Plus, it was just for me, so it felt good no matter how it ended up. I also kept hanging out with my best friend … outside of volleyball, anyway. After a while I started feeling more like me again. I'm not going to pretend it happened all at once. But doing stuff I cared about, even when I didn't really feel like it, made things easier.*

Using her values of relationships, pleasure, and independence to guide her actions, Kat helped herself out of a difficult negative spiral. What was the key to her success? She figured out that she felt best when she was being her *true self*—when she let herself do what she cared about most. You can do the same. Knowing and acting on your values can help you cope with tough times, with the added bonus of helping you to grow into the "you" you want to be.

for you to do

To help reverse your own negative spirals in the future, start by making a personal plan to act on your own values. This plan will include ways to (1) connect with people who make you feel good, (2) achieve goals that matter to you, and (3) enjoy activities on your own.

1. Using the list below, circle one way you can connect with people who make you feel good. You can add other ideas on the blank lines.

   Bake or cook a new recipe

   Go for a walk

   Get a meal/snack

   Sit together and chat

   Talk on the phone

   Watch a movie

   Watch funny YouTube videos

   Listen to music

   Play video games

   Play a sport

   FaceTime/video-chat

   Other: ____

   Other: ____

Plan how you'll connect by responding to these questions:

What activity did you circle?________________________________

What day(s) of the week will you do it?________________________

What time(s) of day will you do it?___________________________

Where will you do it?_____________________________________

How long will you do it each time?___________________________

Who will you be with, if anyone?____________________________

Which values will this activity help you act on?_________________

2. Next, make a plan for working toward a goal that matters to you.

   Write down a long-term goal in an area that reflects one of your top values:

   ____

   ____

   Think of a short-term action that can help you get to this goal. For example, if your long-term goal is "to make or keep relationships," your short-term action might be "visit a new place with a new person" or "do something nice for a friend or family member."

   Plan the details of this action by responding to these questions:

   What short-term action did you think of?______________________

   What day(s) of the week will you do it?________________________

What time(s) of day will you do it? ______________________________

Where will you do it?______________________________

How long will you do it each time?______________________________

Who will you be with, if anyone?______________________________

Which values will this activity help you act on?______________________________

3. Third, make a plan for enjoying an activity on your own.

   Choose your favorite activity from the earlier list. Try to pick something that's easy for you to do on a regular basis.

   Which activity did you choose?______________________________

   Plan the details of this activity by responding to these questions:

   What activity did you circle?______________________________

   What day(s) of the week will you do it?______________________________

   What time(s) of day will you do it? ______________________________

   Where will you do it?______________________________

   How long will you do it each time?______________________________

   Who will you be with, if anyone?______________________________

   Which values will this activity help you act on?______________________________

more to do

Create your final action plan based on your responses above.

1. To connect with people who make me feel good, I will

   do this activity:________________________________

   on these days of the week:__________________________

   at this time of day:______________________________

   for this long each time:____________________________

   and I will be with:_______________________________

2. To work toward a goal that matters to me, I will

   take this shorter-term action:________________________

   on these days of the week:__________________________

   at this time of day:______________________________

   for this long each time:____________________________

   and I will be with:_______________________________

3. To enjoy an activity on my own, I will:

   do this activity:______________________________

   on these days of the week:______________________________

   at this time of day:______________________________

   for this long each time:______________________________

   and I will be with:______________________________

To track your value-based actions, you can download a worksheet at http://www.newharbinger.com/45571. We encourage you to complete this worksheet weekly until your negative spirals become less frequent.

PART 3

View Yourself as a Good Friend

12 brains are wired to jump to wrong conclusions

for you to know

You've already spent some time learning about how amazing your brain is. Your brain can turn the squiggles on this page into words. It can grow and change to let you learn new skills. But even though our brains are pretty amazing, they can still trick us sometimes.

You might be thinking *Wait, what? How would I know if my brain was tricking me? What if it's tricking me right now!* Luckily, learning about brain science can help you understand exactly *when* your brain—despite trying its hardest—might not get things totally right.

It can help to know about the different parts of your brain, and what each of them is built for. One important part of your brain, called the *limbic system,* has several subsections that work together to help you make fast decisions. The limbic system can move so quickly because it looks for patterns and then makes super-quick guesses.

And here's the thing: If it's trying to find patterns in sets of numbers, letters, or most other things, this part of your brain does an awesome job. It allows you to raed tihs wrod and taht wrod wtih no porbelm even though the ltteers are a toatl mses. The limbic system looks at the first and last letters of those words and then makes sense of the rest.

But for more complicated tasks, like coping with stress and setbacks, the limbic system can sometimes give you the wrong idea. Because it's just trying to match complicated patterns really quickly, it can get confused about which actions are most helpful to you. For an example, read Jared's story:

During spirit week at my school, they let us wear hats. Hats normally aren't allowed, so I definitely wore my favorite hat every day that week! I also had three big tests in different classes, and I did way better on those tests than I had earlier in the year. I know it might sound weird, but the next time I took a test in a different class, I felt worried not wearing my hat. Like I had done something wrong by not wearing it? Now, I know my brain had gotten mixed up about which of my actions had helped me do better on the tests. It was trying to tell me it was the hat, but it was actually that I'd been asking some of my classmates and teachers for help more often in those classes.

The limbic system might tell you to do certain things you've done before when you did well—even if those actions had nothing to do with helping you succeed.

for you to do

Think about a time where your limbic system tried to trick you into thinking an action was helpful when it actually wasn't. If you get stuck, you can go back to Jared's story to help you think of an example.

What was your goal in this situation?

____

____

____

What action did your brain (incorrectly!) tell you would be helpful for reaching your goal?

____

____

____

____

more to do

A lot of times when the limbic system messes up, there were other actions we took that actually were helpful. If a friend were in the same situation you just talked about, what would you tell them to do that might *actually* be helpful? These could be things you actually did or ideas you come up with right now. Try to name at least two things that are actually helpful.

13 being kind to yourself helps, being mean to yourself doesn't

for you to know

If you're like most teens, you may feel like you're often under pressure. In fact, teenagers *are* under pressure of all sorts: pressure to keep grades up, to do well in extracurricular activities, and to be popular with peers. Sometimes it may feel like the only way to deal with this pressure is to push yourself as hard as possible. It's common for teens to have thoughts like *If I'm really,* really *tough on myself, maybe I'll get things right.*

It might be tempting to think that being harder on yourself can help you reach your goals … especially when it seems like it works. Maybe you've had the experience of being super harsh on yourself—being self-critical, unforgiving, even mean to yourself—and then getting exactly the outcome you wanted (for example, an A on a math test). You might end up thinking that being hard on yourself was the *reason* you succeeded.

But that couldn't be further from the truth. When you have an important goal in mind, your limbic system (the pattern-matching part of your brain) often matches *being mean to yourself* with *success,* simply because they happened close together. But just because your brain put them together doesn't mean they're really connected. In fact, the best science says that being mean to yourself doesn't actually help. The truth is that being hard on yourself actually makes it harder, not easier, to succeed and reach your goals.

How do scientists know being mean to yourself makes it harder to succeed? Because scientists have listened to and studied experiences from teens across the country—thousands all together. This research demonstrated that teens who are mean to themselves after making a mistake actually feel worse about school and make lower grades over time. Being mean to yourself simply doesn't help you succeed.

Actually, the exact opposite turns out to be true. Research has shown that teens who are kinder to themselves, give themselves breaks, and cheer themselves on end up succeeding at much higher rates than teens who are too harsh on themselves. Plus, kids who are kinder to themselves after messing up—either with friends or in class—have an easier time learning from their mistakes and acting in the ways they hoped to in the future. Basically, science shows that being kind to yourself helps you succeed. It does a better job of telling you how you're really doing. If your brain matches being *mean* to yourself with *success*, it is seeing a pattern that's not really there.

Here's what Jesse, age 16, said:

> *Earlier this year, I had to present my project to the whole class. I was so nervous I would mess up or say something wrong in front of everyone. Each time I made a mistake while practicing, I kept telling myself really mean things. I thought it would make me want to do better, but it seemed to make my anxiety worse, and I definitely felt worse about myself. I was never able to finish practicing, because I was always so frustrated.*
>
> *On top of that, I couldn't even tell how well I was doing on the day of the presentation. Because I kept telling myself these mean things over and over, I pretty much felt bad the whole time I was up there talking. It was impossible to tell if I was doing okay, or if I had truly embarrassed myself or not.*

Jesse's story shows how being mean to yourself can get in the way of reaching your goals. The good news is that because your brain is built for learning and forming new connections, you can change how you treat yourself after you make mistakes. Being kind to yourself after mistakes will get easier each time you practice, as your brain makes new connections.

You can always practice being kinder to yourself to help yourself work toward your goals.

for you to do

During the week, try to notice one time when you make a mistake. It can be a big mistake or a small one, in any type of situation (with friends, at school, or at home). When you notice the mistake, complete the sections below in as much detail as you can..

What happened? Where were you? Who were you with?

____

____

____

What types of thoughts did you have after your mistake?

____

____

____

How did you feel after having this thought?

____

____

What kinder thought could you have about your mistake?

____

____

Take a minute to really think about this kinder thought. How might it feel to try out this kinder thought? Is it *hard* or *easy* to think kindly about yourself? There are no right or wrong answers; just write down your reactions.

____

____

____

more to do

Ask a family member about their personal experience with self-criticism and self-kindness using the questions below, and record their responses. Almost everyone has a story to tell!

Interviewee: ______________________________

Have you ever been self-critical or too hard on yourself? What was going on at the time?

____

____

____

Science tells us that being too self-critical can get in the way of meeting our goals. Why do you think this is the case?

____

____

____

Why do you think self-kindness might help people achieve their goals?

____

____

____

Is it ever difficult for you to be kind to yourself? If so, what makes it easier?

____

____

____

14 build a bridge to self-kindness

for you to know

Even if we know being kind to yourself can make your life better, actually being kinder to yourself might be hard to imagine. The idea of being kinder to yourself might feel, at times, like looking at the faraway side of a canyon. Sure, you can *see* what it might be like on the other side ... but it's fuzzy. The details are hard to make out. And it's not at all clear how to get there.

One of the most powerful ways to build a bridge across that canyon is to bust common myths about self-kindness.

Myth: Being kind to yourself is selfish.

Reality: Being kind to yourself is good for you *and* for others. You'll be better able to help friends with homework, cheer them up if they're down, and cheer them on when they succeed if you show yourself the same kindness you show them!

Myth: Self-kindness is basically the same as self-esteem.

Reality: Self-esteem gets mentioned a lot alongside self-kindness, but they have important differences. Self-esteem is a way of valuing yourself based on others' judgments and judgments about yourself and your performance in various activities (like school, sports, or art). A self-kindness perspective encourages you to value yourself as deserving of kindness, regardless of what judgments others (or even you!) have and no matter how well you performed on a test, in an audition, and so on. The best science we have shows that teens do a better job of bouncing back from hard times (like receiving mean feedback following a practice speech for a class) if they emphasize a self-kindness perspective rather than a self-esteem perspective.

Myth: Self-kindness is mostly about spending lots of money on yourself or doing big, showy things.

Reality: You might see a lot of expensive, glitzy #SelfCare on social media, but self-kindness can be as free and simple as you want it to be. A lot of brands have tried to cash in on young people learning more about self-kindness, and many have tried to rebrand self-kindness as buying their products. Luckily, self-kindness can look like rereading your favorite book, playing with your family's pet, writing down ideas for a new graphic novel you want to start, watching funny videos on YouTube, and lots of other free, easy-to-do activities! There's nothing wrong with buying things as a self-kindness practice occasionally, but knowing which self-kindness activities are free and easy is way more helpful in the long run.

for you to do

In each pair of statements, circle the one that encourages a self-kindness perspective and underline the one that is a self-esteem perspective. As a reminder, a self-kindness perspective says you have value no matter what you or other people say/how you perform, while a self-esteem perspective says your value is primarily about your and other people's judgments about you/how well you perform.

"I know I've made it because I finally ran a mile faster than my goal pace in gym."

"I know I've made it because I'm proud of myself for showing up, even on the days when I don't feel good and can't run as fast as I'd like."

"I know I'm smart because I made As on my last three tests."

"I know I'm good at learning because I've put the work into studying even though the last three tests haven't gone as well as I'd like."

"I'm proud of myself for taking care of me, and now that I've done that I can be a better friend."

"I'm proud of myself because I showed everyone I didn't need to take care of myself."

Which is which? You probably already guessed, but in the first two pairs, the self-esteem perspective comes first and the self-kindness perspective second. For the third pair, the self-kindness perspective is first and the self-esteem perspective second.

It might seem like the self-esteem perspective people are having a better time. But let's pretend those people start having a bit of a harder time. They start running slower, perform poorly on a test, or feel like they do need to ask for help. How do you imagine these people will feel?

____

____

____

How do you think they might benefit by moving from a self-esteem perspective to a self-kindness perspective?

____

____

____

more to do

Challenge yourself to list some ways to be kind to yourself that are free and that you could do nearly every day. If you need help, here's a reminder of some earlier examples: rereading your favorite book, playing with your family's pet, writing down ideas for a new graphic novel you want to start, and watching funny videos on YouTube. Try to list at least three things; then, save them in your phone (or write them on an index card) so you can refer back to them if you get stuck on ways to be kind to yourself!

PART 4

Treat Yourself like a Good Friend

15 recognize your mean thoughts about yourself

for you to know

A good first step to being kinder to yourself is noticing when you are having mean thoughts about yourself. These thoughts can be tricky to recognize if you don't know what to look out for. These clues can help:

Actions: One way to detect mean thoughts is to pay close attention to your actions, or what you're doing (for example, taking a walk or talking to a friend). In the face of setbacks, kind thoughts encourage you to practice self-care activities (like listening to your favorite song, reading a book by your favorite author, or reaching out to a friend). Mean thoughts often discourage you from doing things to take care of yourself, telling you to ignore friends or stop doing your hobbies.

Thoughts: Kind thoughts sound patient and forgiving (*It's okay if that kid doesn't like me. I know plenty of people who would enjoy being my friend*), while mean thoughts often sound impatient or unforgiving (*Why can't I make any friends? I'm such a loser!*). If your thoughts leave you feeling comforted, you might be having kind thoughts—but if they leave you feeling sad, scared, and hopeless, you might be having mean thoughts.

Physical and emotional feelings: Many people who are being mean to themselves have physical feelings (like stomachaches or headaches) that sometimes mean they are in need of extra self-kindness. Others experience emotions like sadness or shame.

Different people use different clues to let them know when to use self-kindness. With practice, you can find the clues that help you know when you're being too harsh on yourself. Here's how Darren, age 14, recognized his clues:

Since I'd always had a tendency to be kind of mean to myself, it was hard to know when it was happening at first. I just always felt a little off. But then, I started to notice a few patterns. First, I noticed I tended to pull away from my friends when I got upset. Like, when even the smallest thing would go wrong or I'd say something awkward, I would stop responding to their texts and just isolate myself. Maybe because I thought I didn't really deserve their support. After that I'd feel so down and lonely, and like there was nothing I could do, or anyone could do, to make it better. My dad once said that I should pay attention to things like stomachaches and headaches as a sort of sign that maybe I'm being too hard on myself, and I should reach out for help. He said that was helpful for him. But that strategy never worked for me, because I don't really feel sadness in my body like some people do. So, to figure out when I'm being too mean to myself, I really have to pay attention to what I'm doing and feeling—like noticing when I feel ashamed, when I think I'm not worth helping, or when I start to stay away from friends.

for you to do

This time, you're the detective looking for clues—specifically, clues that can identify mean thoughts. Ask yourself what let Darren know that he was experiencing mean thoughts.

What *actions* might have let Darren know he was being mean to himself?

____

____

____

What *thoughts* might have let Darren know he was being mean to himself?

____

____

____

What *physical or emotional feelings* might have let Darren know he was being mean to himself?

____

____

____

Put a check next to each clue that helped Darren identify his own mean self-talk.

more to do

Think about a recent time when you felt like you were really mean to yourself after you made a mistake. It could have involved your friends, family, school, or anything else you can think of. Write about what happened:

____

____

____

How did you know you had been mean to yourself? Let's identify your clues in this situation.

Write down any action clues: what were you *doing* when you were mean to yourself?

____

____

____

Write down any thought clues: what were you *thinking* when you were mean to yourself?

____

____

____

Write down any feeling clues: what were you *feeling* physically or emotionally when you were mean to yourself?

____

____

____

Which type of clue do you think will be best at helping you identify when you're being mean to yourself?

____

brainstorm kinder thoughts 16

for you to know

It's one thing to want to be kinder to yourself, but it's a whole other thing to actually do it! Lots of teenagers *want* to be kinder to themselves, but they aren't really sure how to start or what that kindness looks like. The good news is that you get to be the expert on what your self-kindness looks like.

Using self-kindness is a bit like using a toolbox: You never want a toolbox full of only hammers. You often need a bunch of different types of tools (hammer, screwdriver, wrench) to get a wide range of jobs done. Similarly, you'll want to brainstorm lots of different kind thoughts for your "toolbox" so you can use them to help you in many different situations. Having these tools ahead of time means you're more likely to use them when you face a setback. These thoughts should be ones that are believable and helpful for you.

Setbacks often come in a bunch of different shapes and sizes, so the more practice you have generating kinder thoughts, the better. If you're having trouble coming up with kind thoughts for yourself, think about what you would say to a close friend facing a similar setback. Your kind words of support can work just as well for yourself as they would for a friend.

Once Sara, age 14, thought about how she would treat a friend facing a setback, she found it a lot easier to get started:

> *My friends all told me I was being way too mean to myself, but I didn't know what else I could do. When they told me to cut myself some slack and be kinder to myself, I had no idea what that really even meant. How can you learn something new if you don't have any specific examples of it? It wasn't until I thought about what I would do if one of them was having a hard time that it started to make a bit more sense. I made a list of kind thoughts I could use and found the ones I liked most. It felt a lot less weird once I realized I can give myself the same kind of support that I'd normally give my friends!*

for you to do

Here is a list of thoughts that some teenagers had after they made a mistake or faced a setback. Put a check next to each one where the portion in italics is a kind thought. Remember: kind thoughts often involve patience and forgiveness—like the things that you would tell a friend who was having a hard time.

- "I missed getting the grade I wanted by five points ... but *nobody is perfect. If I don't reach my goal, it doesn't mean I'm a bad person.*"
- "I asked someone out on a date, and they said no ... I can't stop thinking about how disappointed I am. *What did I do wrong? There must be something wrong with me.*"
- "Since moving, I haven't made as many friends as I would like ... but *I know there are lots of good things about me, so I'm positive I'll make more friends soon.*"
- "*I'm honestly a pretty cool person* ... it's easy to forget sometimes when I don't get picked for a team, but it's true."
- "After putting off a few of my homework assignments, I feel super overwhelmed ... there's no way I can get all this work done. *How could I let this happen? Maybe I'm just lazy.*"
- "After putting off a few of my homework assignments, I feel super overwhelmed ... then I remind myself *I'm really capable, and I have people who can support me. I believe in myself.*"
- "I was really sad right after my parents divorced ... but *this is a hard situation, and I'm handling it really well. Lots of people would be stressed, and I think I'm doing a good job coping with it.*"

Now that you've identified the kind thoughts above, let's make you the expert. Take a closer look at these kind thoughts—hint: there are five—and rank them from 1 (most helpful for you) to 5 (least helpful for you).

You can use your top three thoughts as a starting point to brainstorming your own kind thoughts. Write down the italicized part of your top three here.

1. ______________________________

____

____

2. ______________________________

____

____

3. ______________________________

____

____

more to do

Here's a list of setbacks some teenagers have faced. For each setback, write down one inner mean thought the person may have had. Then, write down one kind thought you'd recommend instead. For example:

Setback: *I can't get the person I like to notice me.*

Possible inner mean thought: I'm boring; of course they wouldn't see me.

Recommended inner kind thought: I have a lot going for me. If they don't notice me, it's their loss.

Setback: *I'm failing my English class.*

Possible inner mean thought:

____

____

Recommended inner kind thought:

____

____

Setback: *My best friend and I are in a fight, and I said some rude things that I didn't mean.*

Possible inner mean thought:

____

____

Recommended inner kind thought:

____

____

Setback: *I overslept and missed tryouts. I know my coach is really mad.*

Possible inner mean thought:

____

____

Recommended inner kind thought:

____

____

Using your new brainstorming skills, pick one kind thought for yourself. This could be one of the italicized statements from earlier in this activity, one that you wrote for the teenagers' setbacks above, or a new one that you think of now. Write this kind thought down on a sticky note and keep it somewhere you can see it often (for example, a mirror, a computer screen, a door). Use this sticky note as a reminder to practice self-kindness!

17 practice kinder thoughts in the moment

for you to know

While practicing self-kindness *is* helpful, nobody is perfect. It's okay (and normal) to not get it right 100 percent of the time. This means that you'll sometimes catch yourself being mean after a mistake. So what happens when you start to have negative thoughts about yourself when you're stressed?

The answer: you don't give up! Even if you don't feel good at self-kindness right away, it's possible to get much better at it with practice. This means that if you catch yourself being mean, it does not mean you've failed, or that you're "bad" at being kind to yourself. Instead, it just means you have a chance to apply some of the new skills you've learned.

Once you notice you're having mean thoughts, you have the power to change your thoughts from mean to kind. In fact, noticing these mean thoughts means you're one step closer to changing them into kinder thoughts about yourself.

Ava, age 15, felt better after realizing it was okay to catch mean thoughts about herself:

> *At first, I got really discouraged every single time I noticed I'd been mean to myself. I knew being mean to myself was worse than being kind—it seemed like I should be able to stop all those mean thoughts in their tracks. I know it may sound weird, but I started to be mean to myself for being so mean in the first place.*
>
> *It took some effort, but eventually I remembered that self-kindness was something new I was learning. If a friend of mine was learning something new, I'd remind them that learning involves practice and making mistakes. Rather than getting so discouraged, I could use the moments when I was being mean as a chance to try to change what I'd been thinking. Just a few weeks ago, I wouldn't have noticed I'd been mean to myself at all, so I've already made progress.*

for you to do

The column on the left presents mean thoughts some teenagers have had. The column on the right presents mean thoughts that have been changed into kinder thoughts. Draw a line connecting each mean thought to its kind thought.

My girlfriend dumped me. I feel worthless.

I forgot my brother's birthday. I'm the worst sibling.

I failed another quiz. Why can't I get anything right?

My friend didn't eat lunch with me today, probably because she found someone better.

I had a bad day. A friend texted to see if I'm okay. I don't deserve their kindness.

I asked out my crush, and they said yes … but it's just a matter of time until they find out I'm a loser.

Everyone forgets things sometimes! Maybe he'll appreciate me telling him now.

Just because she didn't sit with me today doesn't mean she doesn't like me. Besides, I know I'm fun to hang out with regardless of who sits with me.

If they agreed to go out with me, they probably think I'm cool to start with. That's a big compliment.

I have other people who care about me. I'd tell anyone else they shouldn't be so quick to blame themselves.

If my friend had a bad day, I would definitely check to make sure they were doing okay. I deserve the same kindness for myself.

Everyone has things that are hard for them. Clearly this subject is hard for me. I can try asking my friends or the teacher for help.

more to do

Think about a recent time when you caught yourself thinking really mean things after a setback or mistake.

What were some of the mean thoughts you had? Write down one or two examples:

Now rewrite each mean thought as a kinder thought. (Remember: you can start by thinking about what you'd tell a close friend):

PART 5

Bounce Back from Stress and Loss

18 grow your ability to notice stress early

for you to know

You've already learned a lot of great skills for coping with stress—from this workbook or just by figuring out what works for you day to day. Those skills are super helpful, and you deserve to feel really good about yourself when you use them. And, at the same time, most people we've worked with have said something like Jeremiah, age 14, did: *Sometimes I don't realize I'm stressed until it's already really bad, and it's harder to use my skills once things get bad.*

We want you to know it's common to feel like it's harder to use our coping skills once things are already pretty bad. We can also share two pieces of good news with you:

- You can learn to recognize when you're starting to get stressed out earlier without having to constantly worry you'll get stressed all of a sudden.
- Even if it's a little harder, your coping skills can still be helpful even when you get really stressed out, really sad, really anxious, or really angry.

This activity focuses on helping you better figure out when you're starting to get stressed. The next activity will cover how to use your skills even when your emotions are really strong.

There are two easy ways to notice earlier if you're starting to get stressed: (1) check in every once in a while to see if you're getting physically tenser, and (2) see if there's a pattern to the situations that stress you out.

It's not bad to feel physically tense sometimes. Physical tension can happen after we exercise, and a certain amount is totally normal for people to experience. You might want to occasionally check in to see if you're feeling physically tenser or more "wound up" than usual. An easy way to do this is to notice how close your shoulders are to your ears. The closer your shoulders are to your ears, the more physical tension you're experiencing. You can use this check-in to see if you need to use any of the other helpful coping skills in your toolbox.

It can also be helpful to recognize that some situations might stress you out more than others. You might want to avoid those situations, but if you're prepared to use your skills (maybe even by picking out a helpful skill before the situation starts) you can avoid the stress without avoiding the situation.

Either strategy can help you recognize your stress earlier. It's also okay if you don't catch stress early every time; you can grow these skills through practice, just like all the other skills in this workbook.

for you to do

Let's have you try the shoulder check-in for physical tension right now. If you can, sit straight up in a chair or on the floor. Notice where your shoulders are naturally at first, without trying to move them.

Next, take a deep breath in through your nose for about three seconds and scrunch your shoulders up toward your ears.

Now let a deep breath out through your mouth for about five seconds while letting your shoulders completely relax. You can even shake your arms around a little to loosen them up some.

Notice where your shoulders are now. If they're lower than they were before, you probably had some physical tension and stress. That's okay! Pick one of your favorite coping skills—like talking back to fixed thoughts or acting on one of your values—and use it right now.

If your shoulders are in about the same place, that's okay too. You can use this technique any time you'd like to check in on your level of physical tension. If you do feel physically tense, it might be a good time to use one of your coping skills.

more to do

For the next three days, write down situations that stress you out. Give as much or as little detail as you want for each situation, though you will probably have an easier time with the next step if you describe the situations in a little more detail: *Slept through my alarm, so I had to skip my shower and was late to school* probably will help more than *Slept through my alarm.*

Day 1: ____

____

____

Day 2: ____

____

____

Day 3: ____

____

____

Write down any patterns you notice in which situations were most stressful for you; for example: *I often got more stressed out in the morning* or *I noticed I got stressed if I hadn't eaten in a while* or *I got more stressed out when I had to talk to groups of people.*

____

____

____

Now write down which of your coping skills you'll try to have ready the next time a stressful situation like this happens to you. You can even talk about how you'll use the skill to make it easier on yourself. For example, *I'll try being kinder to myself when I wake up late by asking myself how I would treat a good friend who wasn't a morning person. That way, I can start the day with some self-kindness to help myself not get as stressed out in the mornings.*

____

____

____

get good at getting help 19

for you to know

Dealing with difficult thoughts and feelings can be hard, especially if a large chunk of the stress falls on your shoulders alone. Calling on others for backup can keep you from having to handle it by yourself. In fact, research has shown that social support can make a big difference in helping you feel better when times are hard. Toward that end, it's important to identify your *support circle*—the people you'd feel comfortable asking for help. Here are three significant things to know about getting help:

- It's often helpful to have someone listen to what you're going through. These people can be good friends, parents, aunts, uncles, grandparents, teachers, or anyone else you're close with and trust. Sometimes they may give you a new perspective on what's going on; other times, they may be able to share a time when they felt similarly. In some cases, they may be able to help you reach someone else who can help you more directly—like a counselor or other mental health professional.

- You may not have any friends or family members that you want to go to directly just yet. If that's the case, you may wish to reach out to a mental health professional at school (social workers, psychologists, or counselors). Other times, you may want to talk to someone who has mental health training right away—especially if you feel unsafe or like you might harm yourself. To talk to someone in the United States, you can call the National Crisis Hotline at any time of day or night: 1-800-273-8255. If you prefer to text, you can also text HOME to 741741 at any time of day or night.

- Getting help from others can feel strange at first, especially if you've never done it before. But, just like everything else, it gets easier with practice. The good news is, there's no way to mess up asking for help. No matter how you do it, the most important thing is that you asked for help when you needed it.

Additionally, brainstorming *how* you would like to ask people for help ahead of time may help you do it in the moment.

Here's what Zara, age 16, had to say about asking friends for help:

For a long time, I felt like I had to suffer through everything alone. I felt really sad and hopeless, and like no one else could help me or understand what I was going through. I was even having trouble eating. As I stopped talking with my friends and family, things just kept getting worse and worse.

At some point I decided I couldn't handle it by myself anymore. I told one of my friends what was going on, and how I was feeling. And I felt so relieved! She listened to me for a long time before sharing with me that, sometimes, she felt kind of hopeless too. She asked if there was anything she could do to help me feel better. But, honestly, just having her know my situation was already helping. Now, when I'm feeling especially bad, I know I can go to that friend and get extra support—which is so nice to know.

Other teenagers, like Stephen, age 15, asked for help from a counselor at school:

One day, I just decided I was going to do something about how bad I was feeling. My mood was really, really low, and I was tired all the time. I had a really hard time focusing in class. I didn't know who I could really go to, so I asked my teacher if he knew what I could do. He suggested seeing the school counselor and helped me set up a meeting. When the counselor talked with me, we brainstormed a few things I could do to help me feel better. I'm still working on doing everything that's on the list, but I do feel better knowing I have someone I can talk to when things get difficult.

for you to do

Think of people in your life who you trust and would feel comfortable asking for help. Write their names in the support circle below. People who are most important in your support circle can go toward the center; people who play smaller roles in your circle, but can still offer some help, guidance, or positivity, can go toward the edges. Remember: your support circle can be made up of many different types of people as you want (friends, family, trusted adults, mental health professionals). Choose at least three people to place in your circle.

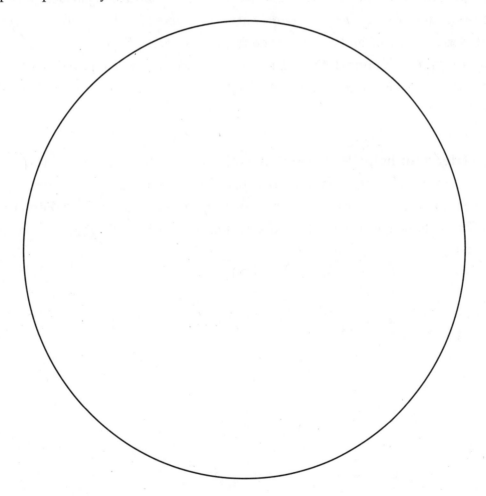

more to do

Now that you've identified people you'd be comfortable asking for help, let's take a look at *how* you'd ask them. Choose three people from within your circle, and write two to five sentences that would explain to each what you're going through and ask them for help. Feel free to use the examples, and remember: there's no right or wrong way to ask for help.

Asking a parent for help: Hey, Mom, can we talk about something important? Lately I've been feeling really sad, and it's been bothering me a lot. It's really hard for me to get stuff done at school, and I've stopped having fun doing things I normally enjoy—like hanging out with my friends. I think I need to change some things to help me feel better, but I'm not sure where to start. What do you think about my seeing a counselor at school?

Asking a friend for help: Hey [friend's name], maybe you noticed me pulling away from you and the other kids lately? It's not because I'm mad at you or anything. I'm just having a really hard time right now. I've been feeling really sad, and it's been bothering me a lot. It would help if I could talk to you about some of it. Can we talk for a bit?

Now try it out using your own words. Be sure to write one for each of the three people you chose.

Person 1: ______________________________

____

____

____

____

Person 2: ______________________________

____

____

____

____

Person 3: ______________________________

____

____

____

____

20 grow gratitude

for you to know

When you feel grateful for someone or something, it's your brain's way of telling you what you want or need. For example, think about the last time you were *really* groggy and tired. Now, think about how grateful you were for that night's sleep. The gratitude you felt was your brain's way of telling you "Sleep is important; please rest more!"

Growing your gratitude is like drawing a road map pointing to the people, places, and things that make your life better. Anyone can grow their gratitude, but it may take some practice at first. These tips can help you get started:

- You can be grateful for people, places, and things. Sometimes gratitude means feeling grateful for a *person* who's there for you when you're struggling. Other times, you may feel grateful for a particular *place* you can go to relax. Or you may feel grateful for a *thing* that helps you get through the day—like your music, your books, or your soccer practice. There are lots of ways to grow your gratitude.
- Being grateful doesn't mean you have to forget about difficult things going on in your life. In fact, paying attention to gratitude when you face obstacles helps you find new ways of coping with tough situations. Instead, being grateful means not letting the challenges you face—like stress about schoolwork, trouble with friends, or negative emotions you might be having—get in the way of what you want or need. Especially when things are hard, gratitude can guide you toward people, places, and things that can help you cope with whatever is going on.

Amir, age 15, shows how gratitude can help find new ways to cope:

> *I used to think about self-harm sometimes. The thoughts were hard to ignore, especially when I was by myself and not around my friends. One day, I played some loud music to help distract me. I ended up leaning back, closing my eyes, and focusing as hard as I could on breathing with the song that came on. My music helped me make it through each breath until the moment passed. I was grateful for the distraction, and that told me I should try using my music the next time. Having a plan helped me feel like I had more control of the situation.*

for you to do

Read Li's story, then respond to the questions that follow it.

My sophomore year in high school, my mom lost her job. Money was really tight, and I knew we were struggling to afford things even though my mom tried to keep it from me. I was constantly worrying about all the bad things that could happen. What if we couldn't keep our house? What if I had to change schools? I really didn't want to move away from all my friends.

I was able to tell at least one of my friends how worried I was about moving away and losing our friendship. She promised me we would still be friends, no matter how far away I was. We talked about how often we'd call each other, and I felt a little better. But on other days, I didn't feel like being around anybody. On those days, I went for a walk in the park behind my house. It was super peaceful there, and it gave me time to think and to get away from it all. I'd even bring a book with me sometimes and read outside. Reading helped calm me a little, too.

Six months later, my aunt offered to let my mom and me move in with her. We could sell our house, but only had to move two streets away! I was relieved because it meant my mom could save up the extra money while looking for a new job … and I didn't have to leave my friends. It did mean I had to share a room with my mom, but at least I could keep hanging out with my friend! I loved visiting her house, especially since it gave me some extra space outside of my own cramped home. It can be hard to have space when you're sharing a room with someone, but I quickly learned I could create a little bit of personal space for myself by putting in my headphones and listening to some music. The headphones were a nice way to let my mom know I needed some time by myself, which she seemed to understand. With everything going on, I think she liked having some time to herself, too.

Who's one *person* Li may be grateful for? Why do you think Li is grateful for this person?

What's one *place* Li may be grateful for? Why this place?

What's one *thing* Li may be grateful for? Why this thing?

Now try growing your own gratitude. Think about one person, one place, and one thing you're grateful for. Make sure to include *why* you are grateful.

Who's one *person* you're grateful for? Why?

What's one *place* you're grateful for? Why?

What's one *thing* you're grateful for? Why?

more to do

Now follow your gratitude road map to share your gratitude with others. Think about the person you named above. Write a letter to this person, explaining why you are grateful for them and how they change your life for the better. If you'd like help getting started, use this template, or download it at http://www.newharbinger.com/45571. Once you've finished writing, you can either share your letter with them … or keep it to remind yourself to keep growing your own gratitude.

Dear ______________________,

I just wanted to let you know I'm very grateful for you. I really appreciate you because

____

____

____.

You make my life better by

____

____

____.

Thank you,

____

(your name)

concluding thoughts: to the future you

You've come a long way! You've learned about (and seen) how and why you have the power to change, even when you feel like you don't, in ways you might have never considered. Depending on where your mindset change plan led you, maybe you've learned how to talk back to your fixed-mindset thoughts in ways that feel right and true for you. Maybe you figured out what you value in this world—what matters most to you today, what might matter tomorrow, and how to keep acting on your values in everyday life. Perhaps you've taken steps to be kinder to yourself, even though being mean is what came naturally in the past. You've tried out practicing gratitude and getting help when you need it (everybody does at one time or another). You've reflected on how to cope with setbacks and get back on your path toward getting what you want from life, all while becoming the "you" that you hope to be.

If that sounds like a lot to accomplish, it's because it *is* a lot, no matter how you say it! Sure, you might still have a way to go on your growth-mindset journey. Maybe you haven't fully reached the goals you wrote down back in Activity 8. That is completely okay. In fact, it's exactly what we'd expect. Every big change begins with small steps. No step is easy, but every one counts. With every activity you completed in this workbook, you took a few small steps toward real, tangible goals that you have and will continue to achieve.

So now, as you consider what steps will come next for you, please first take a pause to feel proud. Proud of yourself for the steps you've taken, the journeys you've started, and the many you'll take in the future.

How will you continue to grow and change in the future?

Write a letter to Future You—the you of one year from today—to share what you've learned by going through these activities, and what lessons you hope you'll continue to carry and act on in the future. Which obstacles have you started to overcome? What strategies helped get you there? What advice do you have for Future You as you go through new stressors, setbacks, and obstacles in the future?

Help your future self continue to grow by sharing your real thoughts, feelings, and advice right now.

Jessica L. Schleider, PhD, is assistant professor of psychology at Stony Brook University, where she directs the Lab for Scalable Mental Health. Schleider completed her PhD in clinical psychology at Harvard University, her doctoral internship in clinical and community psychology at Yale School of Medicine, and her BA in psychology at Swarthmore College. Her research on brief, scalable interventions for youth depression and anxiety has been recognized via numerous awards, including a National Institutes of Health Director's Early Independence Award; the Association for Behavioral and Cognitive Therapies (ABCT) President's New Researcher Award; and Forbes's "30 Under 30 in Healthcare."

Michael C. Mullarkey, PhD, is a postdoctoral fellow at Stony Brook University. He previously completed his PhD in clinical psychology at The University of Texas at Austin, his doctoral internship in clinical psychology at Stony Brook University, and his BA/MA in psychology at American University. Mullarkey has been recognized as a Bridging Barriers Fellow and the Top Student Researcher in the Mindfulness Special Interest Group of the ABCT. He has partnered with nine high schools and colleges to test and disseminate single-session interventions for depression and anxiety.

Mallory L. Dobias, BS, is a clinical psychology PhD student at Stony Brook University, with a BS in psychology from The University of Texas at Austin. Dobias has contributed to the development and/or dissemination of six different mental health interventions for depression and anxiety. Through intervention research, she disseminated an online growth mindset program to over 2,900 students in seven Texas high schools, and developed her own first-authored intervention program that is now undergoing research evaluation at the Child Mind Institute in New York City, NY.

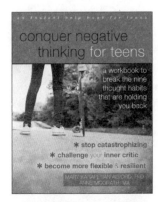

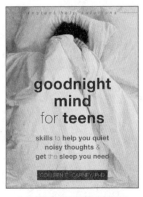

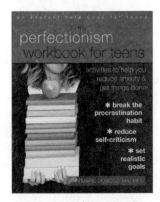

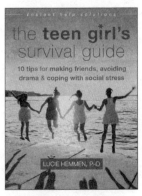

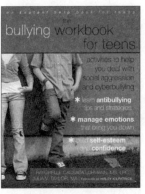

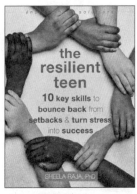